The Catholic Church and American Culture

Reciprocity and Challenge

edited by
Cassian Yuhaus, C.P.

preface by
Donald S. Nesti, C.S.Sp.

PAULIST PRESS
New York/Mahwah, N.J.

Library of Congress Cataloging-in-Publication Data

The Catholic church and American culture : reciprocity and challenge / edited by Cassian Yuhaus.
    p. cm.
    Includes bibliographical references.
    ISBN 0-8091-3153-6
    1. Catholic Church—United States—Membership. 2. United States—Civilization. 3. United States—Church history. 4. Christianity and culture. I. Yuhaus, Cassian J.
    BX1406.2.A645   1990
    282′.73—dc20   90-31316
                                            CIP

Published by Paulist Press
997 Macarthur Boulevard
Mahwah, New Jersey 07430

Printed and bound in the
United States of America

Contents

Preface

Donald S. Nesti, C.S.Sp.

We are all aware that the whole creation, until this time, has been groaning in labor pains. And not only that: we too, who have the first-fruits of the Spirit, even we are groaning inside ourselves, waiting with eagerness for our bodies to be set free (Romans, 8:22–23).

Ours is, indeed, a world that is groaning for fulfillment. For the first time in the history of humankind we are able to look at it from two perspectives—as "insiders" and "outsiders." We are able to place ourselves both in its "inner space" and also remove ourselves to its "outer space." From the perspective of a space ship the azure-white sphere which is Earth appears to be benign and peaceful, small, fragile and vulnerable. It is our home. From that outer space, beyond the earth's atmosphere, we are able, at least physically, to go beyond all cultural, political and other boundaries and immediately realize that we are all inhabitants of one home.

As "insiders" living within the earth's physical atmosphere we know that we are free agents who can either create or destroy both our ecosystem and our cultural "atmospheres." In creating or destroying either, we are creating or destroying ourselves and humanity; for both are contexts in which we grow to fullness as persons or we die. But there is still another sense in which we can apply the distinction between "insider" and "outsider" to the reflections offered in this book.

All of the authors who have contributed to this work are themselves seriously concerned with the physical well-being of our world and its environment. They give their attention more specifically, however, to reflecting on the freedom that allows us to adopt and create our American culture and how this American culture affects

our lives. As inheritors and participants in our culture—"insiders"
—these authors presume the presence of God's grace within American culture, no matter how seminal it may be. As persons who have
been asked to bring a more transcendent eye to an analysis of our
way of life, and how it must yet be transformed by love, they do so
as participants in a community of faith which enables them to take
on an "outsider" view of the realities that we face. One can easily
recognize in their reflection that their experience has involved both
the agony and the ecstasy, the travail and birth, that we Catholics
and fellow Christians feel as we yearn for the fulfillment of our true
identity and as we are confronted by the reality of the cockles and
the wheat present in our daily lives.

As "insiders" we seek to describe with as much hard-nosed
realism as possible the light and shadow sides of our culture; as
"outsiders" we attempt to bring the infinite light of the gospel to all
that is less than fully human or is disrespectful of the goodness of
God's creation. St. Thomas Aquinas so clearly and simply stated,
"Gens humanum arte et ratione vivit" ("Humanity lives by creativity and intellect").[1] As subjects of culture we are struggling with the
question of our identity as a society of persons who share a commonly held way of life—world-view, beliefs and notions, norms
and standards of conduct, shared meanings, symbols, codes of interaction and communication. We, self-reflective, finitely free and
essentially relational human persons create our culture/ways of life
and are responsible for their conforming completely to the mysterious love of the Father.

Never before in history have peoples and cultures been challenged to become peoples without frontiers as they are today. The
diffusion of technological and economic systems, the groaning of
entire peoples for the democratic process, the profusion of instant
information and communication through media and computing,
the vast movements of peoples emigrating and immigrating, and
much more, demand that we look beyond our own boundaries and
allow the process of the compenetrations of cultures to take place.
At the same time, we feel the tremendous need to live and proclaim
the good news of God's love, the experience of which alone is
capable of empowering us to choose ultimate transcendence. It is
true that, at times, we feel overwhelmed by what seems to be an

unending process of growth and change, of constant adaptation, of being uprooted and of seeking a deeper base of our identity. It may be, however, that all of these phenomena are ways in which humankind is impelled and catapulted into a meditation on the true universality inherent in the gospel message. Are not the global examples cited above the creations of free human persons; are they not cultural realities which relentlessly express groaning for fulfillment in the universal call of Christ who commands us to love as he did? Are they not the results of the use of our power which at the same time exercise their power over us?

Ever since the Second Vatican Council began to struggle with the question of relating the mystery of the gospel and the church to the contemporary world, the church, in a multiplicity of cultural settings, has been involved in an ongoing process of self-reflection and self-evaluation. Given the historical context in which the Council took place, the church undertook a deeper and more thorough self-analysis than ever before of its relationship to itself, to the contemporary world and to God. In a word, it undertook a reflection on the mystery of its being, of its mysterious identity. In doing so, it chose to look lovingly at all aspects of reality, the divine or the human, at itself and all with whom it relates. Nothing could be more demanding or satisfying than this: to take a quiet, leisurely and relaxed look at who you are; to make sure that the look is creative and generative of life; and to have the wisdom to listen and wait with creative patience for growth and transformation to take place freely. It was this attitude that pervaded all of the documents of the Council. For our purposes, it is especially important to note that this attitude underlay the Council's statement on the church (*Lumen Gentium*) and the church in the contemporary world (*Gaudium et Spes*). Furthermore, that same Council invited all members of the Catholic community, other Christians and all persons of good will to enter into this leisurely, loving look at themselves and their cultures in relation to the church's defense of the dignity of the human person and cultures. That same invitation of the Council continues to beckon, invite and challenge us to meditate in like fashion.

Is it any wonder that the problem of identity becomes more and more complex and its solutions seem to be more relative, given the number of options that people and societies in the Western world have to determine what they want to be and to do. The sense of individual and cultural self-determination and power that we possess leads us to believe that any way of life that we create for ourselves can be justified. And even we as Catholics immersed in this cultural perception often forget that the *essential criterion* for the ways of life that we create, individual or societal, is the person of Christ and his unconditional love. The sometimes painful process of trying to grasp and distinguish what is essential to the nature and mystery of the church from what is time bound and accidental, how the incarnation of the gospel message and its living out within a given culture is colored by the cultural context, forces us to look at all aspects of our lives as a Christian community in the world: our vision flowing from our relationship with the risen Christ; our belief system; our notions about all aspects of life; and finally the way that we call each other to live out that relationship according to the norms and standards of mutually acceptable action on behalf of justice, peace and a preferential option for the poor. At every point along the way, we are called upon as church to seek and give the meaning of Jesus Christ to whatever culture and way of life that we freely create and share. We know that every people attempts to answer three basic questions and, thereby, give meaning to their existence: 1) What is wrong with life? 2) What ought the good life be like? 3) How does one bridge the gap between what is wrong and what ought to be? Nothing can be more challenging, exciting or anxiety-filled depending on an individual's or a society's sense of security about its identity. In some ways it would seem that the easiest thing to do would be to ignore the questions, and the process of self-reflection that they involve, by attempting to create a kind of time capsule. To do so would be cultural suicide. Rigidity and exaggerated defensiveness rob a way of life and its symbolic systems of the credibility, the intelligibility and the internal authority which they must have to allow a people within a culture to relate to the signs of the times.

Cultures are living realities because they are the ways of life of living human persons. They are inherited but never fixed, ever in motion and experiencing new infusions of life. So, too, is the process of inculturation of faith within a given way of life. That is why it is so necessary that appropriate care be given to nourishing the life of faith within one's culture. Without taking time for this, meaning becomes confused, symbols lack credibility and intelligibility and norms and standards lose their internal authority. Living faith means dynamic life. A truly inculturated faith possesses both an openness to change as well as a legitimate defensiveness against what would destroy its meaning. This is what necessitates a constant dialogue between faith and culture rather than antagonism. It also requires an asceticism of discernment which must be at the heart of the dialogue.

To discern the nature and role of the Catholic intellectual community within American culture requires that we be doggedly honest, clear-eyed, and able truly to listen and be truthful. Such a project of discernment is not for the faint-hearted or the easily shaken. Those who undertake the process must believe deeply the words of Jesus when he says that you *are* light and you *are* salt. Both of these are declarative statements and not mere hortative constructs. We only contribute to the darkness and insipidness if we choose to do so by refusing to share the light and savor of our gifts. To discern is to sift and to test the spirit and meaning underlying our American culture, to read its symbolic systems, to judge the messages it communicates and its actions. To discern is to look at the fruits that our thoughts, "habits of the heart" or attitudes and behavior bear.

The challenge that this presents to the church, and the Catholic intellectual community in particular, is immense. It means that the church will be ever-conscious that it is God's Spirit dwelling within the community that leads its corporate discernment process. This is particularly true and necessary in relation to the present universal and incomprehensibly precipitous movements towards new and restructured global political, economic and social relationships, all of which present us with ambivalence and dilemmas and whose ultimate outcomes are not clear. American culture itself must seek new clarity concerning its role in relation to the unjust distribution of wealth which continues to worsen internationally and domestically.

We are also aware that while technology continues to bring us to a level of material well-being never before seen, it simultaneously threatens the quality of our lives in so many ways; that while the dignity of the individual human person is so highly prized, grossly exaggerated individualism and emphasis on individual rights stretch human relations to the breaking point; that while equal opportunity is constitutionally assured all persons to seek life, liberty and happiness, the self-esteem of vast numbers of our citizenry is desperately low and in many cases non-existent. Is it any wonder that so many Americans are enslaved to drugs, that so many of our youth are despairing, and that permanent commitments in marital or other relationships seem to be so impossible? When it comes to education, the rhetoric of government and other officials praises the theoretical value of education in itself, while the reality is that the outcomes of our systems of elementary and secondary education declare their virtual bankruptcy. Nor should we fail to mention the pervasive temptation of higher education to sell its soul by becoming a feeder system for training personnel that respond to the demand of the labor market rather than developing *personae educatae* who will be prepared to contribute to the commonweal.

These are not new problems; nor are they articulated here for the first time. I cite them simply as a way to whet our appetite for the pages that follow and the contributions that the authors of the coming chapters make to our process of discernment. These chapters constitute part of the proceedings of a conference which was held for presidents of Catholic colleges and universities at the College of St. Catherine, St. Paul, MN, in late 1988.

Given my tenure and experience as president of a Catholic university, I was aware that it was rare for presidents of Catholic institutions of higher learning to gather at conferences or symposia to reflect on a subject such as faith and culture. For the most part the topics of conferences for presidents tend to focus on any one of a number of administrative, legal or budgetary concerns. This is true simply because the presidents' time and energy are heavily consumed by these daily concrete realities and preoccupations. Only infrequently do they have the opportunity to gather with their colleagues for a substantially long enough period to reflect on the more philosophical, theological and cultural dimensions of the educational project.

Approximately a year and a half prior to when the conference at St. Catherine's was held, we began consulting a broad spectrum of persons about the feasibility of holding a conference specifically for Catholic college and university presidents on the topic of: "The Church and American Culture in the Post-Vatican II Era: The Challenge to the Catholic Intellectual Community." This consultation included some thirty individual presidents of Catholic institutions, the Pontifical Council for Culture, The Association of Catholic Colleges and Universities, the National Catholic Education Association, and the Association of Jesuit Colleges and Universities. The response of them all to the idea of such a conference was overwhelmingly positive. Both the Pontifical Council for Culture and the ACCU agreed to cosponsor the conference whose stated goal was "to be a collaborative proving toward discerning an agenda of Catholic intellectuals concerning the church and American culture, as we enter the second generation after Vatican II." Some ninety presidents actually attended the three-day meeting and represented the rich diversity of Catholic institutions of higher learning: smaller liberal arts colleges, women's colleges, larger comprehensive universities, institutions of local, regional and national outreach.

The conference program was designed on the model of a zoom lens. It allowed the participants to move from a broader, more general view of the relationship of Christianity and Western culture, to a more specific purview of Catholicism in the history of American culture. This was followed by an analysis of the American way of life today, its central cultural metaphors and attitudes, a reflection on the Protestant experience of faith within American culture and, finally, it looked to the future of the interaction between the American cultural ethos and Catholic vision, values and community. The chapters that follow basically incorporate these contributions.

In the first chapter, David O'Brien seeks to elucidate several of the ways in which Catholics have historically participated in making and interacting with American culture. His presentation presumes that Catholics did not always agree on the style which they should use in making their unique contribution to American life. While the historical circumstances evoked the development and use of these styles, the styles continue to exist side by side in healthy tension even to this day. He identifies three distinct styles of this interaction which are based on as many understandings of the relationship between Catholicism and American culture: 1) the *republican* style which felt at home with American pluralism and whose strength lay in its sense of civic responsibility; 2) the style of the *immigrant* church which sought to respond to the question of how Catholics could be effective "outsiders" within the culture; and, 3) the *evangelical* style, which relied on the strength of vision and prophetic witness and focused on personal commitment to Jesus Christ. Each in its own way sought to protect the integrity of the faith by separation from the culture.

In the second chapter, Margaret Steinfels undertakes an analysis of the subject of American Catholic intellectuals: Are there any? Who are they? Where are they? How have they/how do they see their role vis-à-vis church and culture? What kind of agenda should the Catholic intellectual community draw up for itself as it faces the future? Her development of the material reflects, in a sense, some of the same points raised by O'Brien but strictly with the present situation in mind. She clearly counters the dangers of anti-intellectualism within the Catholic community and extends a strong call for all its participants—theologians, those who possess the charism of the magisterium, and other intellectuals in the broader community—to enter into dialogue on faith and culture. She cautions that such a dialogue can only be effective if the participants are willing to enter into it with full academic rigor and deep mutual respect for all voices as they seek further insight about the question of Catholic identity and American culture.

John Coleman, in chapter three, brings the resources of a highly skilled anthropologist to this process of discernment. He is specifically concerned with the light and the shadow sides of the American way of life. He accepts the metaphor of the "market place" as dominant in our way of life and begins with Calvin Coolidge's premise that: "The business of America is business." He develops an appreciation of the three dimensions of "American commercial democracy" which we, as Americans, live and breathe: *consumerism, technology,* and *individualism.* After sketching the general contours of a theory of culture, he assists the reader in developing an appreciation of the strengths and weaknesses of the three. He discusses how each of the three detrimentally affects the development of the truly human and concludes by proposing a short agenda which would allow the Catholic intellectual community to assume leadership in achieving "a moral unity of discourse and vision" now absent in American life.

The perspective of the professional theologian is the contribution of Monika Hellwig. She undertakes the task of proposing a theological point of departure for the dialogue between faith and culture for the next decades. With courage, she attempts to articulate a prophetic voice even more than do the other contributors. As we know, prophets often say things which people are reluctant to hear, in a way which is not always pleasing. They are rarely accepted "in their own country." Her concern is that all the participants in the discernment dialogue consciously recall the fundamental truth that all human persons have been created in the image of God as finitely free, intellectually reflective and essentially relational. She urges us not to fear what American culture, with its focus on freedom and its tradition of British common law, can teach the church about respect for human rights and the use of human freedom. If the church were to take these strengths and gifts of American culture seriously and apply them to the democratization of church polity it would enhance the quality of the relationships of those involved in the dialogue of the Catholic intellectual community and, in turn, lead to an appropriate and powerful inculturation of the faith in our culture. Conversely, the church's principal strength in confronting American individualism-run-wild is its belief in the "communal nature of the human situation in terms of creation, sin and redemption." Only faith in these will lead to the experience of gratitude and adoration as the only remedy to unbridled independence.

Hervé Carrier helps us reflect on the Western phenomenon of "Modernity" and "the process of modernization" as it affects not only the Western and first world, but how its effects have been exported and have spilled over into the developing countries. Its principal danger lies in the way it tempts the West to perceive itself as "the soul of the world." He recalls the rich insights of Vatican II in *Gaudium et Spes* and the clarity with which it described the ambivalence of the effects of modernity.

Catholic discernment about faith and the American experience would be totally amiss were it not to include a contribution to the dialogue from the Protestant tradition which was at the very heart of the creation of the republic. Martin E. Marty stimulates our thought by touching on key elements in the experience of the Protestant heritage. He describes the development and ratification of the Constitution as a summary statement of much of the covenanting heritage so central to Protestant tradition and our beginnings. This statement allowed a broader latitude in the understanding of *Foedus* (covenant), thereby permitting the incorporation of more sectarian groups into it as well. He also notes that the later period of immigration in our history brought about a tension and insecurity as Protestantism struggled to understand its role in relation to the new "outsiders" and their place within the *Foedus.*

Anyone reading these chapters will understand how the original presentations by the authors stimulated an abundantly fruitful dialogue among the president-participants in the conference held at St. Catherine's. As leaders of the intellectual community, they recognized and accepted their grave responsibility not only to participate in the process of discernment that the authors had begun but also to extend the clarion call to do so to the larger Catholic intellectual community. It was with a sense of excitement and enthusiasm that they entered the dialogue to discuss such topics as: 1) the future agenda for the Catholic intellectual community; 2) the agenda for presidents of Catholic institutions of higher learning; 3) the leadership which they needed to provide for the discernment concerning the relationship between faith and culture. The brief amount of time that they had would not permit them to develop a consensus response to these questions. Nevertheless, it was clear by the conclusion of the conference that there was strong commonality in the insights, desires and concerns that surfaced in the small discussion groups in which they had been configured. Even though space does not permit our developing a comprehensive list of these concerns, it is enlightening to look at some of the more prominent ones. They are an example of what can happen once the spirit of discernment takes hold of larger circles of participants within the Catholic intellectual community.

In response to the question about the principal challenges fac-

ing the Catholic intellectual community in America in the 1990s
and beyond, the presidents recognized that we still must learn both
how to stand "within" and "outside" our culture and develop new
moral and ethical frontiers for American society. This, they said,
would require the raising of consciousness of the actual and potential members of the Catholic intellectual community concerning
their role as thinkers in the church and in the broader American
intellectual community. The presidents also discussed some of the
most critical aspects of their role as leaders within their institutions
in order to accomplish this. They mutually extended a strong call to
each other and to other colleagues to reexamine their institutional
missions in light of Catholic identity and American culture. This,
they felt, was at the heart of the process necessary to develop a
renewed academic community. They clearly understood that this
would lead further to a review and possible revision of curricula
which would respect both faith and culture. They candidly expressed concern that they find ways to keep themselves intellectually alive and to seek ways and means to encourage intellectuals
to be supportive of one another. It was important to them that they
be seen as the spiritual leaders of their institutions and that they
spearhead and maintain the process of evangelization within them.
One of the most difficult and perplexing points raised was how to
remain prophetic as institutions and at the same time remain finan-
cially solvent; no one is more aware than they of the many audiences they serve and the many sensitivities and points of tension
that arise within and outside the Catholic community as they seek
to relate faith and culture.

In their reflection on the identity and agenda for Catholic intellectuals, one group described the Catholic intellectual as "a reflective practitioner whose habits of the heart and mind are informed
by Catholic Tradition." Their agenda which they foresaw can only
be undertaken by persons of hope and fortitude. It requires that
they have a proactive attitude toward cultural change. Some of the
agenda items which they cited were: the development of a renewed
appreciation of scholarship for its own sake by encouraging research, publication and lecturing; the development of a group of
Catholic intellectuals who would address problems arising from the
encounter of faith and culture and which would serve various au-

diences and groups with their expertise. The presidents also felt that it would be the responsibility of the Catholic intellectual community to raise consciousness about Catholic cultural concerns at state, regional and national levels.

Finally, they discussed how they, themselves, might address better the issues which they had raised. Foremost in their view is the need to network among themselves and with other college presidents. They also felt a strong need to be educated more extensively regarding faith and culture. They specifically called upon the ACCU to act as the vehicle to assist them in accomplishing these two tasks. Some suggested that a "think tank" be formed to furnish presidents with food for thought on issues that were raised at the conference. They also realized the need to educate trustees, administrators and faculty on the relationship of faith and culture.

It is my earnest hope that the pages that follow will have the same catalytic effect on the reader as it did on the participants at the original conference. It is my firm conviction that there are many other representatives of the Catholic intellectual community who have been reflecting on the same questions, feeling the same tensions, experiencing the same longings and desires in attempting to rediscover the meaning of Catholic faith for today. This book and the presidents' conference which produced it are clear evidence of the Spirit-filled collaboration which alone will develop an adequate and clear Catholic world-view about the human person, the world and God. Only a communal response will be strong enough to incorporate the valid insights and values of our culture and at the same time challenge the as yet unredeemed aspects of our way of life. Ultimately what we proclaim is that the only way to God is through the human, and that those who do not know God can never know fully the nature of the human person.

Note

1. St. Thomas, commenting on Aristotle, in Post. Analyt., n.1.

The Church and American Culture During Our Nation's Lifetime, 1787–1987

David J. O'Brien

INTRODUCTION

In the last year or so "Bloom County" has replaced "Peanuts" and "Doonesbury" as my major source material on religion and American culture. Today's topic reminds me of a strip a year or so ago in which two of the junior age characters are lounging in a rubber raft on a summer afternoon. One murmurs: "My life needs spirituality. Yep. That's it. I need religion." After a moment's reflection, he continues: "But which one? I mean, there's a lot riding on this." "Checked the yellow pages?" his friend asks, but the seeker ignores him. "Its a consumer's nightmare. Too many brand names." His helpful companion comments: "I wouldn't take any chances," and, nodding, the seeker responds, "I'm joining 'em all." So there it is, pluralism and the agony of choice. "Life is a test," says the preacher in "Kudzu," another popular comic strip. "I know," responds his teenager parishioner, "but I prepared for true or false and it turned out to be multiple choice."

We are here to discuss Catholicism and American culture, and the reader of comic strips is tempted to say we've got it wrong: it's Catholicisms and American cultures. Andrew Greeley has discovered what he calls "selective Catholicism" and "do it yourself Catholicism." A new experience for Catholics, perhaps, but as old as the Second Congregational church in any New England town. When the Great Awakening, the first of the great revivals, swept the colonial churches, congregations divided and some walked out, to start another. A few years later and any student of the gospel could take to the circuit and begin it all again, like Alexander Campbell and his friends restoring primitive Christian simplicity, or William

1

Miller warning of the second coming in the virgin forests of the new world, while the learned Emerson told Harvard's would-be divines to trust their experience and come out from settled establishments. And that was just the beginning of a journey whose latest landmarks include not only Protestants ranging from Jimmy Swaggert to a handful of married Catholic priests who once were Episcopalians, but, wonder of wonders, Ralph Diorio and Daniel Berrigan and knots of fundamentalists who happen to be Catholic. Once we attributed the chaos of American Christian sects to the inevitable workings of the Protestant principle of private judgment. Pluralism, at least within the ranks, was their problem. No longer. Catholicism and American culture: we might try the Catholic yellow pages.

It is not only religion that is bewildered by pluralism. Our commentator today can be no more confident that we know what we mean by "American culture," certainly not if that person is an historian. Perhaps it is reflective of our continuing rediscovery of pluralisms that American historiography presently is highly fragmented; there is no widely accepted synthetic interpretation of American history as a whole. In the 1960s the post-World War II interest in national character and consensus gave way to a renewed emphasis on conflict and diversity. One result was a sophisticated social history focused on minority groups and local communities. Cumulatively, these studies have deepened knowledge of popular experience and popular culture, and broadened interest in the family, religion, race, ethnicity, and the role of women. They have undercut earlier progressive and consensus approaches to American history, but as yet have produced no synthetic revision, with the result that history no longer plays an important role in shaping either popular or elite understandings of contemporary American life.

For the historian, then, generalizations about American culture prove extremely hazardous. A generation ago the concept of culture provided the theoretical underpinning for some creative works which emerged from the American Studies movement. However, the turmoil of the 1960s, and especially the upsurge of interest in black history, women's history and working class history, along with the turn to "community studies," first in colonial history and later in studies of nineteenth century industrialization, exposed the imprecise manner in which students of history and literature had offered generalizations about the American people and their symbols. Influenced especially by anthropologist Clifford Geertz, the new social history examined many American cultures, local ways of life unified around common symbols, leaving us with a bewildering mosaic. The relationship between those subcultures and American institutions as a whole has remained largely unexamined, at least by historians. Those who have taken the risk present a portrait of complexity, even of contradiction, as Americans seem at one and the same time individualistic and conformist, tolerant and intolerant, materialistic and idealistic, the most religious and the most secular of peoples. The reaffirmation of pluralism, based on more concrete, bottom-up readings of American experience, makes students of American history and culture wary of generalizations about national values, institutions and character, including the self-interested generalizations coming from religious bodies. But, for the moment at least, it also leaves them with few constructive contributions to dialogue about national values or national policy.

American Catholic history has exploded in quality and quantity in the last generation, but its very explosion is part of the larger problem. The turn away from national history has led to an upsurge of interest in social groups located at the bottom of the social ladder or outside what was once taken to be the mainstream of American life. Urban, immigrant, and working class history, along with studies of emergent industrial society, necessarily drew attention to the heavily Catholic European immigrants who filled the factories and the new industrial neighborhoods. The same movement toward subsections of American society has made historians of American Catholicism more comfortable with a focus on Catholics rather than on the relationship between Catholics and the larger society. Exploration of parishes, schools, religious beliefs and practices, and institutional organization no longer appears as parochial but as part of the wider movement of concrete, grass roots, bottom-up writing of American history. Moreover, because so little work was done on American Catholics until the last two decades, historians of American Catholicism are able to utilize the interpretive framework of adaptation of European practice to the American environment associated with progressive history. Thus an early church relatively at home in the United States gives way to an immigrant church notable for its separation from mainstream culture until in very recent years the population and the institution become finally Americanized. This interpretive framework, for all its richness, takes little note of the fundamental challenges to an approach which presumes the existence of a mainstream and questions the criteria which judge some groups "American." Indeed, the very explosion of American Catholic history, with its uncovering of coherent local cultures notable more for their self-conscious construction than for passive resistance to modernity, is part of the challenge. Nevertheless, it is possible to discern in that emerging historiography at least three distinct understandings of the relationship between Catholicism and American culture, each reflective of specific dimensions of the historical legacy, each contending today in the life of the American church. Each turns upon distinctive perceptions of American culture, and each suggests a different approach to the church's own pastoral development.

The American experience of pluralism has shaped the unique public presence of the church in the United States. The heart of the matter was self-consciousness. In the more integrated, traditional societies of Catholic Europe before the nineteenth century, the church had a clear public role because it was an official church; parish and civic birth and marriage records were one and the same; in one way or another the church enjoyed public financial support; it ordinarily controlled education, provided necessary social services, and was the custodian of the community's moral life. The state for its part had a religious character. Kingship was surrounded with religious symbolism, political authority was sanctioned by divine mandates, and, in the years prior to the formation of the new church in the United States, the governments of most European Catholic countries effectively chose bishops, controlled publication of papal and episcopal decrees, and even attempted to determine the location of churches and schedules for religious services.

What this reflected was a traditional society in which participation in the church and participation in the wider community were not considered distinct. By the end of the eighteenth century, however, the sphere of religious and secular were beginning to separate. Already struggles were taking place over censorship, finances, ecclesiastical courts, and education, and these would become more severe, culminating in the outbreaks of anti-clericalism which punctuated the French Revolution. By the nineteenth century, the problems posed by modernization, often accompanying urbanization and industrialization, threatened the hegemony of the Catholic Church and posed choices for individual citizens. Religion, like it or not, was becoming more and more a matter of personal decision, which is to say that affiliation with the church, and the quality of affiliation, were becoming matters of self-conscious decision.

So it was for American Catholicism after John Carroll launched the new church in 1789. As a minority, Catholics found the challenge of pluralism particularly intense. Providing priests and places of worship, educating children and relieving the needy, buying land and building centers of community life, all required people, money and motivation. When hundreds of thousands of immigrants began to arrive, the organizing, unifying and educating of Catholics became an even more deliberate process. It is hardly surprising that the American church appeared preoccupied with itself. Non-Catholic Americans worried that the church's success in organizing its people would divide communities and endanger the precarious experiment in self-government, while European Catholics had the opposite fear, that their American brethren would become too American, too concerned with buildings, money and quantitative measures of success. Both concerns were justified to some degree, but each reflected a lack of appreciation of the dynamics of the American religious environment. Bishops and clergy had little choice but to segregate Catholics to some degree from other Americans if the church was to survive as an identifiable community of faith; thus the appearance of separatist strategies and language emphasizing the distance between Catholicism and other elements of American culture. But they also had little choice but to accommodate to the basic institutional imperatives of the United States if it was to survive as an American church. Thus the frequent claim that Catholicism was not only compatible with American culture but even provided the surest foundation for the American democratic experiment. The church was a minority, in some sense an outsider, in a country perceived as Protestant, but it was also one minority among many, led by confident, successful men who had no intention of withdrawing into a ghetto. As Laurence Moore has pointed out, they manipulated insider-outsider language, appearing now as the victim of nativism, now as the authentic defender of American freedom, in an ever changing struggle to strengthen their own community's internal coherence while avoiding confrontation with their people's aspirations for liberation from the age-old burdens of poverty and powerlessness.

First, this produced a *republican style*, creatively outlined by early leaders like John Carroll and John England, rendered a minority stance by the waves of nineteenth century immigration, revived by John A. Ryan and liberal Catholics of the twentieth century. It achieved its finest formulation in the work of John Courtney Murray and is represented today by the effort to shape a "public church" seen in the recent pastoral letters of the American bishops and the thought of scholars like John Coleman, S.J. and Rev. J. Bryan Hehir. This position begins with positive endorsement of church-state separation, religious liberty and religious pluralism. These endorsements reflect a deeper affirmation of modern culture rooted in a sense of being at home in the modern world, in this case in the culture of the United States. The American Catholic church thus must be fully itself, fully Catholic, and at the same time it must be fully American, accepting in principle and practice the demands of personal freedom, religious pluralism and democratic culture. Republicanism resists sectarian definitions of Catholic faith and identity which overemphasize the distance between Catholicism and American culture and marginalize the church in public debate. Shaped by the enlightenment, by the experience of the early Anglo-American Catholics and by notable converts from Yankee America, it grasped the fact that the individual Catholic was both Catholic and American, that there were tensions between the two, but that on the basis of reason and mutual respect one could be fully responsible to both. Its paradigm, to use a modern term, was the relatively successful middle class Catholic laity, so faithful to the church that they could not understand themselves apart from it, but fully at home, or at least wishing to be fully at home, in their community, their nation and their world. At times, as when facing persecution or its threat, or when caught up in the heady experience of economic and social advancement, the republican Catholic rigidly segregated religious and civic loyalties, urged the church to stick to religion, and engaged in economic and political life with no direct and little indirect reference to religious faith. At its best, in John Carroll or Isaac Hecker, the republican tradition recognized the tension between religious and civic allegiances and attempted to mediate between them, asking what America had to teach the church and what the church could offer to America. In more concrete terms, lay middle class Catholics helped priests, bishops and religious build the church by organizing, educating and disciplining the poor immigrants, and they told their neighbors this was an obvious contribution to civic welfare. They also took part in civic affairs with broad good will, concern for the common good, sincere dedication to American ideals, and occasional suggestions that the church had something important to offer the community.

The other two styles of relating Catholicism and American culture represented a split in the republican inheritance. If the latter mediated between the internal preoccupations of the church and the secular concerns of the public, the immigrant tradition, assisted by the ultramontane movement in Europe, gave church needs and interests the priority. Inside the church, this tradition has always been present, for churchmen, after all, have dedicated their lives to the church and sincerely believe it is the means through which men and women can attain salvation, so that personal considerations and truth itself demand that priority attention be given to religious values and interests. In the United States the threats posed by external hostility and internal diversity, in a setting in which money and personnel were always inadequate, reinforced the drift toward a more self-interested form of public presence. Many of the church's own members were immigrants and working people. On both scores of class and nationality, they were at the bottom and outside the dominant culture, exploited to a degree, looked down upon as well. The United States was a nation with very weak public institutions. Local and state government did little to relieve poverty, even at times of panic and financial dislocation; nor did they do anything to ease the process of adjustment for newcomers to the badly governed, almost anarchic cities. What institutions did exist were for the most part in the hands of native-born non-Catholics. Many of these immigrants were peasants who had few illusions about public life; they knew that life was hard, that power mattered, and that rewards came to those who were shrewd, tough-minded and dedicated to their own survival. Thus they adapted well to the marketplace of interest group politics and to the economic marketplace where power determined rewards. The more ambitious among them took the lead in organizing ethnic associations, often with churches at the center, both to preserve old world traditions and to facilitate advancement in the new, and the organizing skills they exhibited there spilled over into political machines and developing forms of trade unionism. Samuel Gompers' business unionism and the bread and butter liberalism of the machines were expressions of the immigrant style, an American form of interest group liberalism. Self-interested ecclesiastical politics, measuring men and measures by the perceived well-being of the church, was simply another form of this interest group approach. The immigrant church, like its immigrant people, tended to view the world from the perspective of its own interests and ideals, and to use what power it could muster to protect itself, to promote its interests, and to demand respect for its ideals.

Forged by early Irish leaders like John Hughes and carried forward by prelates like Bernard McQuaid, William Cardinal O'Connell and George Cardinal Mundelein, the immigrant style often seemed associated with old world conservatism, an image reinforced by the Americanist crisis when conservative American leaders and Rome rejected republican strategies, but Hughes and later churchmen were sincerely and outspokenly patriotic and deliberately and self-consciously modern in their approach to institutional construction. Embodied in the day to day practice of most American Catholics, this style was initially shaped by the combination of the immigrants' need to preserve old world traditions and the resurgence of American nativism. Both undercut the sense of being at home associated with Anglo-American Catholics, American-born converts, and better educated, more assimilated immigrants. Peasant cultures from which the immigrants came, their own earlier experience of pluralism and urbanization in Europe, and the demands placed on families and communities by migration combined to sharply separate the way of life of family, church and ethnic group from that of the larger community. Reinforced by a conservative piety and ecclesiastical policies aimed at forming practicing Catholics, this experience led to the creation of sharply demarcated Catholic subcultures, held together by sacramental and clerical discipline. Meaning came to be centered on this subculture, while the larger world of economic and political life was rendered morally dangerous and religiously indifferent. America was affirmed as a land of freedom and opportunity, but criticized for its materialism, individualism and permissiveness, a selective evaluation based more on group and institutional needs than on systematic evaluation of cultural practices. Nor did such selective negative judgments stand in the way of active efforts to secure economic advancement, social status and political access; indeed the piety and pride associated with the distinctive world of Catholicism laid solid foundations for dealing with the contentious pluralisms of American life and the marketplace metaphors by which they were understood.

The immigrant style was reflected not only in group centered approaches to public policy and pastoral practice by church officials but in machine politics, business unionism, ethnic activism and a hard-nosed, bootstraps, self-help ethic which informed the Catholic sense of public morality. Some historians continue to see the Catholic subculture as alienated, not yet Americanized, an archaic ghetto of old world values doomed to give way before the educational and economic advancement of its members. Thus the continuing description of contemporary American Catholic history in terms of the Americanization of the immigrant church. But the fragmentation of American historiography, with its resulting challenge to all descriptions of an American mainstream, allows more sophisticated analysts like Timothy L. Smith to contend that these communities were themselves already quite American. By this view, immigrant Catholicism, like the republican Catholicism which preceded and regularly challenged it, represented an appropriate response to the problem of being both Catholic and American, that is, being themselves while bearing responsibility for the common life now shared with others. Most important, this latter view, like so much of the new social history, sees immigrant Catholics and their ecclesiastical leaders as active and responsible agents in shaping their history, in contrast to the image of passive adaptation once common in discussing immigrant peoples and institutions. This latter interpretation makes it easier to understand why the immigrant style persists in a post-immigrant church, for it is still necessary to shape a distinctive sense of peoplehood in a context of pluralism. Echoes of this approach are heard today in the church's intimate association with trade unionism and community organizations, its organizing strategies among new immigrants, and its persistent support for "bread and butter" liberal social policy, as well as in the backing of some bishops for a traditional, interest-group approach to moral issues like abortion and self-interest issues like tuition tax credits. The immigrant style has two outcomes, a subcultural restorationism aimed at recovering the unity and integrity of Catholic peoplehood and developing a distinctive Catholic public agenda, and a comfortable denominationalism which uses republican language to perpetuate the segmentation of religion and public life which confined religious meaning and authority to church and family while leaving the laity free in economic and political affairs.

The third Catholic public style reflected the other side of the tension between Catholicity and American pluralism. For some sensitive Catholics the republican style was too secular, the immigrant style too selfish. Neither, it appeared, had much to do with Christianity or with the life and witness of Jesus. They could not be satisfied with the subculture which the church's leaders constructed in order to preserve the faith and insure institutional survival. Neither were they satisfied with the dualism of a republican tradition which, by the time industrial society arrived, tended to segregate religion from the rest of life and reinforce the modern schism which historians have noted as part of the experience of Christianity in the modern world. Instead they sought a reintegration, personal, communal and public, by means of a complete commitment to the gospel, expressed in profound religious faith, an interiorization of the spiritual life, and a dedication to serving the poor and healing the wounds besetting society. Found first among founders of religious orders and a few idealistic lay people, this strand emerged in the Catholic Worker movement of Dorothy Day and Peter Maurin. Practicing voluntary poverty, experimenting with utopian alternative communities, and, later, offering a witness of Christian non-violence to war and the arms race, the Catholic Worker represented the appearance of an evangelical style in American Catholicism. Relegated to the margins of a church organized in the interest group style and a culture dominated by new manifestations of the republican tradition, evangelical Catholicism would begin to spread in the wake of Vatican II, the race crisis, the war in Vietnam and the deepening spectre of nuclear annihilation. While few Catholics would join the Catholic Worker or the various resistance and counter-cultural movements that sprang up around it, many responded to a spirituality which called for fundamental commitment to the gospel and witness of Jesus and resulting distance from contemporary culture.

Through two centuries of organized existence in the United States, then, the American church evolved at least three distinct understandings of its public role and responsibilities, and the three came into open conflict in the 1960s. The majority of Catholics were for the first time in a century politically unmobilized, uncertain of the character of Christian commitment in a Catholic framework, and confused about the relationship between their Catholic inheritance and their public and daily experience. Internally the new voluntarism left in the wake of renewal forced the exploration of new pastoral strategies. Top-down educational programs designed to reeducate Catholics after Vatican II foundered on ideological conflicts and lay indifference. Radical strategies, spawned by groups as diverse as traditionalists, charismatics, and peace and social justice activists, called the church to recover its integrity by opposing the obvious corruptions of the larger society, ignoring the web of personal and family needs which had always underpinned American congregational life. A variety of movements indicated that many of these needs were not being met, while shrinking numbers of priests and religious indicated that change would be needed to attract individuals to church service. The result was a bottom-up, rather loose, pastoral style, seeking to encourage men and women to define their needs and find the resources to meet them, while providing training and support for a variety of new forms of ministry. In dioceses, parishes, apostolic movements, and church based institutions, the need to generate voluntary support, lay leadership, and human and financial resources also led to a greater sharing of responsibility evident in team ministry, lay dominated advisory boards, and pastoral planning based on widespread participation. All of this drew individuals, whether full-time church workers, volunteers, or simply members, to the kind of participation once hinted at among lay trustees. It also made the church more public, as its actions and decisions, subject to debate and various forms of deliberation, achieved legitimacy through participation.

The church had also become public in another sense. The bishops were now heavily involved in public debates about government policy. They spoke out on a wide variety of foreign and domestic issues, and in some cases even testified on behalf of specific legislation. These statements in the two decades after Vatican II constituted a large volume, climaxing with the major pastoral letters of the mid-1980s. In presidential election years the bishops have offered testimony to the platform committees of both parties and issued "political responsibility" statements to the faithful, setting forth their views on a broad range of issues, listed without priority among them. In 1976, attempting to enlist broad support for the social mission of the church, the bishops sponsored the Call to Action process to which I have referred. The democratic process, which saw a lay person having the same vote as a bishop, and the progressive nature of the resolutions made many members of the hierarchy nervous, so that its results were more or less shelved. But the program signaled changes which could not be reversed. Both the church's internal vitality and external integrity depended upon participation and consent; the public church was more than a phrase.

In the debates which have taken place it has become clear that the three distinct approaches to American culture have persisted, but the balance among them has shifted dramatically. The most dynamic and influential is now the evangelical. Catholic faith and piety, like that of other American Christians, is increasingly centered on the scriptures and the person of Jesus. Pastoral approaches to baptism, confirmation, marriage and adult education increasingly feature invitations to personal commitment and decision. While public debates continue to feature discussion of papal teaching, doctrinal formulas, church documents and catechetical materials are less significant than the scriptures and works of piety which emphasize Christian discipleship. And, as happened among Protestants, social responsibility has come to be seen in personal terms. The question was less "what does the church teach?" than "what would Jesus do?" Naturally enough the demands of religious faith and church membership are seen as challenging conventional values and practices, establishing new boundaries for the church not so different from the old. Whether it was a charismatic oriented lay person worried about drugs, sexual promiscuity and abortion or a Catholic Worker worried about militarism and poverty, the response was similar: personal conversion, detachment from a corrupt society, and commitment to the community of faith. Touching the heart of faith and establishing the distinctive ground of the church, this approach has enormous appeal and moral force. In their 1983 pastoral on nuclear weapons the bishops came close to affirming this position by emphasizing the dramatic demands of the gospel, affirming non-violence as an option for individuals, and calling their people to discipleship in a "society increasingly estranged from Christian values," indeed a society in which they might expect persecution and martyrdom to become normal. In their later pastoral letter on economics, they refer to the phrase popular in Latin America, "the fundamental option for the poor," as reflective of the demands of discipleship and the priorities for the church, once again set over against a society seen as materialistic and selfish.

The reason for the resurgence of this more radical language is clear. In 1961 *America* magazine published an article justifying the use of force to keep neighbors from invading one's fallout shelter in the event of nuclear war. Writing to peace movement leader James Forrest, Thomas Merton exclaimed: "Are we going to minimize, and fix our eyes on the lowest level of natural ethics, or are we going to be Christians and take the Gospel seriously?" John Courtney Murray's advanced version of the republican tradition had been modest; he had pointed out that natural law ethics provided no leverage for bringing about the kingdom of God, only for establishing minimal levels of decency. Neither did it provide an emotionally compelling ground for resistance to evil. Indeed Murray himself had argued that because limited nuclear war might be necessary, it must be justified. Merton posed his question about this "lowest level of natural ethics" and asked about the gospel in 1962.

In the years that followed he and others would ask similar questions about racism, about the Vietnam war, about world and domestic poverty, and finally about the nuclear problem, by the 1980s seeming to carry the very fate of creation. In the face of such issues, the republican style, for all its strengths, seemed inadequate.

The strength of the evangelical approach is its appeal for integrity, calling the church and its members to live out their faith and thus witness to the demands, and the truths, of Christianity. Like the Catholic Worker movement, it exposes the impersonal character of the state, condemns a spiritually empty pursuit of material self-interest, opens prospects for spiritual and social renewal, and expands the social imagination to embrace all human persons, including society's outcasts and unfortunates, and to a vision of a world of personal responsibility and mutual self-help. Like all radical movements, the Catholic Worker has been marked by "a fierce adherence to a fixed set of ideas, a focus on final ends rather than changing conditions, and a willingness to endure political failure and to stand alone if necessary." It presents a necessary challenge to the concern of other movements with effectiveness. "We believe that success, as the world determines it, is not the criterion by which a movement should be judged," the Worker maintains. "We must be prepared and ready to face seeming failure. The important thing is that we adhere to these values which transcend time and for which we will be asked a personal accounting, not as to whether they succeeded . . . but as to whether we remained true to them even though the world go otherwise." Such evangelical Catholicism inspires dedication and sacrifice seen in the tremendous variety of projects serving poor, homeless and powerless people, challenging the arms race, and opposing American policy in Central America and the third world.

Its weakness is that, by defining issues and responses in Christian terms, its advocates become marginalized in the larger public debate. Respected, even admired, they are not seen as offering an appropriate or reasonable way in which the American public as a whole can evaluate problems and formulate solutions. Only part of the problem is church and state. Rather it is a problem of responsible citizenship. If social problems are at least in part problems of power, organization and institutions, and if they almost always intersect with government policy, a pluralistic society simply cannot deal with those problems in specifically Christian terms. Nor can the individual citizen effectively participate in the public debate, persuade non-Christians, or indifferent ones, or influence the larger culture by appealing to the authority of the gospel. Evangelical Catholicism taken alone, then, challenges the church, but limits the audience, restricts the language and short-circuits responsibility, tending toward a perfectionism, even an apocalyptic sectarianism which, by always questioning the legitimacy of secular institutions and policies, devalues the demands of citizenship and reduces the moral significance of work, politics and wider community life. At its worst, in the watered down version which has worked its way into popular piety and educational materials, it slips into a soft sentimentality which excuses inaction on public issues by arguing that until people decide to be good, reform will not work. "That one should work first for the moral reform of individuals before seeking political and economic reform is altogether too simple and superficial," John A. Ryan told a friend discouraged by economic and racial injustice. "Those who advocate this course are either persons who haven't taken the trouble to analyze the possibilities and implications of the moral reform proposal," or who don't really want reform at all.

The second approach to American culture, the immigrant style, did not disappear with the assimilation of European immigrants. In fact it has experienced a revival among newer immigrants, most notably Hispanics, but also including a growing number of Asiatics. Echoes of older church battles are heard in demands for foreign language parishes, while older forms of grass roots mobilization take place around parish based community organizations. Community organizing, grass roots empowerment of poor people and minorities through self-help organizations built upon neighborhood, ethnic and racial groups, or people suffering a specific form of powerlessness, remains the major form of Catholic social action and reflects the legacy of Catholic experience in parishes, political machines and trade unions. Unfortunately, there had been little theological reflection on this uniquely American form of social action, nor on the business unionism and bread and butter liberalism so strong in the American Catholic tradition.

Church teaching on social issues is caught between evangelical and republican approaches; from both of those perspectives, community organizing, like self-interest politics and conflict oriented unionism, seems to unduly compromise either Christian or civic ideals. Disdain for this dimension of the American heritage reflects a continuing ambivalence about democracy in Catholic thought, and a failure to come to grips with politics with a small "p" among evangelicals and republicans alike.

There is another, more visible expression of the immigrant style, one that also persists in the American church. John Hughes was the first to mobilize Catholics for public goals, and later church leaders, while professing to be aloof from politics, occasionally used their implied political influence to seek aid for parochial schools, to resist changes in legislation regarding birth control, or to insure that Catholic interests were respected in welfare and education legislation. While opposition to abortion attracted considerable non-Catholic support, the strategies used by activists reflected this approach. In 1968 Cardinal Krol of Philadelphia seemed to favor the election of Richard Nixon because of his support for aid to private schools; four years later he and several other bishops leaned in Nixon's direction because of his professed opposition to abortion. Four years later, despite public statements that insisted on a multi-issue approach to the election, the bishops aroused widespread criticism by appearing to test candidates Gerald Ford and Jimmy Carter on the basis of their view of abortion. In 1984 several bishops similarly challenged the abortion views of vice presidential candidate Geraldine Ferraro and New York governor Mario Cuomo, both Catholics. In the states, abortion, homosexuality and the school issue continue to arouse Catholic leaders and pose the threat of a Catholic vote. Conservative writers like James Hitchcock even contend that Catholics should develop and promote their own agenda of family and sexual issues and demand respect for these specifically Catholic concerns in the political arena.

The strength of the immigrant style is its recognition of how often the moral dimension of an issue is irrelevant in practice. When Americans differ over the morality of a problem, that problem cannot be resolved by government; only when a widespread national consensus was developed was civil rights legislation possible. In the absence of such consensus, issues are resolved by the relative power that groups can exert in the legislative and administrative process and on public opinion, which shapes the parameters of institutional behavior. And, as Michael Novak once learned, public opinion, more broadly culture, is itself an arena of combat. This was the wisdom of the Legion of Decency; recognizing that officially imposed censorship would be unacceptable, the movement mobilized Catholics and used boycotts and publicity to influence decisions within the film industry. In the economic sphere, the problem of unionization was not resolved by a moral decision of the government to recognize the right to organize, but by labor mobilization, posing a threat to labor peace, community order, and successful anti-depression policy, while taking advantage of an anti-business climate to influence public opinion in a pro-union direction. Neither the evangelical emphasis on gospel fidelity nor the republican emphasis on civic-mindedness faces the problem of power in a pluralistic society, nor does either have an evident strategy to in fact bring about changes in policy.

The weakness of the immigrant style is self-evident. To the faithful evangelical, it seems cynical: what would Jesus have to do with organizing, conflict and confrontation, or with hard negotiation about competing interests? To the republican, the immigrant style seems divisive and self-interested, Madison's factions expanded beyond property to include social, cultural and moral interest groups as well. The labor or community organizer and the lobbyist for business seem equally abhorrent to the citizen concerned with the public good. When the church acts from the immigrant, group centered perspective, therefore, it is compelled to escalate the moral language, making the issue it promotes seem to be directly related to Christian belief, and therefore to paint opponents as anti-Catholic or anti-Christian. It also must argue that its position corresponds with the public interest, that what is good for the church is good for the community. In either case it risks appearing self-righteous and authoritarian, and often appears more concerned with vindicating its own rights and commanding recognition than with doing something about the issue itself. On an issue like abortion, when it becomes defined as a Catholic issue and a test for the Catholic politician, the church ends up in the same position as the evangelicals, marginalizing its voice and restricting its potential influence by the sectarian strategy of loyal witness whatever the cost.

Finally, there is the republican approach, extending from John Carroll and John England to John Courtney Murray and, today, Cardinal Bernardin. Acknowledging as always the sharp separation of the religious and political order, the bishops use the Vatican II formula that the church has no specific agenda of its own but seeks to defend human dignity, promote human rights and contribute to the unity of the human family. The two styles of teaching outlined in the peace pastoral brought the republican tradition up to date, and also showed the influence of the evangelical revival. One style, addressed to members of the church, begins with the message of Jesus and explores the responsibility of Christians and of the church. The second, aimed at the general public, is intended to contribute to the development of the public moral consensus, to influence public opinion, and to help shape the public debate about policy by clarifying its moral dimension. Here the language is that of natural law, human dignity and human rights. In other words, within the church the evangelical style is dominant, in the public debate the republican style is required. The tone of the theological and pastoral discussion is radical and demanding, tending toward non-violence and calling for a separation from those values and practices in society which contradict the gospel. The bishops again endorse conscientious objection, including selective objection, they warn military officials against performing immoral acts, and they challenge employees of defense firms to question whether their work can be reconciled with the demands of faith. The public sections of the document, in contrast, are carefully nuanced, their conclusions tentative, the language guarded, most dramatically in the "strictly conditioned moral acceptance of deterrence." In similar fashion, the economics pastoral three years later, in its several drafts, moved from a Vatican II emphasis on work in everyday occupations as the locus for the pursuit of holiness by enhancing human dignity to a more evangelical emphasis on family and church as repositories of counter-cultural values standing in opposition to the dominant values of American society. Once again there are serious policy proposals and appeals for ethical behavior, but the religious language and symbols are confined largely to church.

Church teaching thus struggles between the evangelical approach of Dorothy Day and the republican approach of John Courtney Murray and John A. Ryan. But the disputes about these approaches appear irrelevant to the experience of most Catholics. Lay Catholics remain largely unfamiliar with church teaching. Pastors are only slightly more conversant with the teaching, and often sadly lacking in the knowledge of public issues Ryan thought so necessary. Lay Catholics tend toward an evangelical sense that personal conversion and personal morality are at the heart of the Christian community, and its fruits are measured by being as decent as one can in a hard, amoral world. The tendency of evangelical Catholicism is to devalue everyday life to the extent it is lived amid contemporary institutions; if one does not join a radical community, renouncing ordinary secular existence, then the church tends to become a refuge, an alternative, a counter-culture standing in negative judgment on the world, and therefore on the worldly part of the lay person's life. The republican style tends toward another kind of separation between the church and everyday life; by looking upon Christian existence in evangelical terms and public life in terms of natural law ethics, and not religious meaning, it can contribute to the very separation of religion and life it seeks to overcome, and play into the hands of those who regard the intrusion of the church into public matters as inappropriate.

The American church has always had a dual task: to be itself a credible witness to the gospel and to participate with others in shaping public opinion and forming the public conscience. This must mean that the laity, "citizens of two cities," are at the center of the church's life and mission. John Courtney Murray argued that the church-state question had been transformed from an institutional question to a question of conscience, so that Christian influence on public life depended less on the institutional church and the hierarch than upon "the quality and credibility of Christian witness in secular society." Father Bryan Hehir places the pastoral letters in this context. The church's ability to influence public policy on arms or economics, Hehir argues, depends on its "capacity for moral persuasion of its own community and of the civil community." The goal is to make of our church "a community of conscience, a body of citizens with a commitment to human rights and a concept of social justice which allows them to make concrete judgments of where and how to stand on questions of legislation, social policy, and specific choices facing their neighborhood and nation." To reach this goal, in turn, there must be "a constant process within the church of articulating and examining the public dimensions of faith." For this to happen, all of us must become convinced that "issues of public policy are the business of the Christian community as part of our faith commitment." In short, lay Catholics must form their consciences in church and bear responsibility to carry faith into daily life. Not until the layperson, seeking to live with integrity as a Christian and responsibly as a citizen (the Catholic member of the school board, the Catholic executive, labor leader or social worker, rather than the Catholic Worker or the lay director of religious education), becomes the center of pastoral attention and theoretical reflection will the dichotomy between evangelical separatism and republican accommodation, each so self-serving for the church and so counter-productive for its public mission, be overcome.

In 1983 the United States Catholic hierarchy published their widely discussed pastoral letter on nuclear weapons, "The Challenge of Peace: God's Promise and Our Response." To prepare the letter, the bishops consulted with experts and, for the first time in history, distributed drafts of the letter, encouraging commentary from interested parties. Naturally enough, those drafts caught the attention of government officials, leaders of other churches, and the media. While Catholics were examining the drafts in parishes, schools and diocesan offices, the bishops and their letter were being featured on the evening television news and in the Sunday newspaper supplements. As a result, the letter became a public document, as well as a church document. It rekindled a national debate on the ethics of nuclear policy and the arms race as well as a church debate on the requirements of Christian discipleship.

Interested Catholic citizens found themselves involved in two types of dialogue. One took place when they discussed the issues of war and peace with their fellow Christians; then talk centered around what was required of them as followers of Jesus Christ and members of the Roman Catholic communion. The second took place when they discussed the latest reports about the arms race with other people, some not Catholic or Christian, at work, at parties, or in public meetings; then the dialogue revolved around the responsibilities of citizens of the United States living in an interdependent and dangerous world. For some, perhaps, there was little difference between the two experiences. A person might, for example, argue that the conclusions of the civic discussion are binding on the Christian: what is required by the nation sets the parameters for what the church and the believer must do. In its crudest form this means that "religion has nothing to do with politics." In more sophisticated terms, set most clearly by the great Protestant theologian Reinhold Neibuhr, moral persons live in an immoral society, so that Christian moral ideals may be binding on individual conscience but they cannot become normative for collective groups or for the state. The other way to avoid a problem relating the two conversations is to reverse the priority, arguing that what is binding on the Christian is also binding on society. This was the approach of an older version of the Protestant social gospel which asked simply, "what would Jesus do?" It shows up today in its simplest form in demands that Christian moral obligations regarding sexuality be taught in public schools or even enforced by law. Its more sophisticated form is expressed by theologians as the demand that the church and each Christian witness to the moral demands of the gospel and recognize that, because of the depth of contemporary pluralism, it is simply not possible to shape a public morality, much less live by one, without compromising the integrity of Christian faith. There are other ways to avoid the problem of the two debates. Church people can refuse to take part in the public conversation, or citizens can ignore the religious and moral dimension of the issue. Or one can engage in both but simply refuse to relate the two: of course the gospel makes serious demands, but of course we must be realistic.

To their very great credit, the bishops recognize the problem. In the letter they described "two styles of teaching" in the contemporary church. One, addressed primarily to Christians, begins with shared faith in Christ and explores the demands of discipleship. The other begins with the common moral norms of all citizens, most importantly the dignity of the human person, and explores the demands of citizenship. There are two distinct but overlapping audiences addressed, Catholics and all Americans. The letter has two

purposes, to help the church and its members form their consciences on war and peace, and to help shape the public morality on
the basis of which public decisions about public policy are made.
Finally, the letter uses two languages, or types of discourse, one
Christian, the other more broadly human. The tension between the
two runs through the letter, exemplified by setting side by side
passages which uphold non-violent love as the better way and
others which define a "strictly conditioned moral acceptance" of
deterrence. The striking honesty of the letters, unique in modern
Catholic documents, is matched only by its audacity. For the bishops want nothing less than to find a way of dealing with this issue
which allows the church and each person to live with integrity, with
their actions matching their beliefs and values, and to live as well
responsibly, sharing with all other Americans in making decisions
about a common life. It is the most direct, forthright encounter with
the problem of pluralism in the history of American Catholicism.

One suspects, on the basis of the historical record and this
analysis, that in the future public Catholicism will not be contained
exclusively in any of the three approaches. The force of evangelical
Catholicism will undoubtedly grow as the realities of voluntarism
assert themselves more fully among Catholics. Republican ideals,
with their separation of religion and secular culture, have always
dominated episcopal political thought; they seem inseparable from
the experience of pluralism. The immigrant style will persist as long
as there are groups in need of power and recognition, and as long as
the church feels insecure about the integrity of its witness to its
specific values. One suspects, in fact, that the immigrant style has a
continuing attraction. Republican ideals of democracy and human
rights, carried into the church, threaten ecclesiastical authority and
risk the unity and discipline of the church, as the bishops learned in
the trustee dispute and are learning again in dealing with women.
Evangelical ideals, testing everything in the church by gospel standards, also threaten to undermine episcopal power and open the
door to an egalitarian church. The immigrant style tends to affirm
grass roots organizing and empowerment of the poor while maintaining the internal structures of the church; it poses no threat. Thus
bishops like George Mundelein and Robert Lucey were highly
authoritarian in dealing with their priests, and with theological and

moral teaching, but powerful champions of the working class in one case and of Mexican Americans in the other. The combination of ecclesiastical conservatism and social progressivism is in greater continuity with the past than the other positions, and could receive strong reinforcement as Hispanic Catholics become a more significant element within the church.

Yet one hopes that this will take place in a constructive way to lessen the tension between evangelical and republican positions. Each represents something important: integrity, responsibility and effectiveness. If the center of attention is the laity, standing within both church and society, a better, richer theoretical framework and a more effective pastoral style might emerge. In any event there can be no escape from public Catholicism, for even a religion which professes to confine itself to spiritual matters by that very stance influences the larger society. Whether the development of public Catholicism is constructive, making a substantial contribution to the nation and the universal church, or simply further fragments the American church and weakens its witness and influence, depends, in the end, on attitudes toward history, toward the human community, and, most important, toward American society and culture. If Catholics and their church can learn to understand and appreciate their history, if they can come to feel that this land, where they live, is their own, for which they are responsible, if they can come to see themselves as part of an American as well as a Christian people, then they may indeed help enliven public life and restore a sense of public responsibility in American institutions. The story of American Catholicism is not yet finished. The next chapter remains to be written.

Beyond Assimilation: Let's Get Wise

Margaret O'Brien Steinfels

For most of our history—Catholic history—in America, the larger culture has set our agenda. Our ancestors left Ireland, Italy, Germany, Poland, to finish with an agenda of poverty, hunger, landlessness, religious discrimination, and move onto an agenda of opportunity, jobs, food, land, and freedom. Many of our great-great-great grandparents, grandparents, perhaps parents, did not achieve those goals, but we are the beneficiaries of their hard work and faithfulness to that agenda.

American Catholics now enjoy a level of affluence, of influence, and of power that exceeds the wildest imaginings of those immigrant grandparents. We are assimilated. We are the mainstream. We are the people our parents warned us against.

I want briefly to scan that history and the history of the discussion of Catholics and intellectuals in order to direct our attention to four questions which, summed up, are asking: What kind of agenda should the Catholic intellectual community draw up for itself as we pass into the twenty-first century?

I will do that by talking about three books, two experiences, three definitions, three temptations, and three suggestions.

The discussion of Catholic, American, and intellectual has been long, mostly honorable, and usually disheartening. I begin, as many do, with Monsignor John Tracy Ellis in 1955. Monsignor Ellis opened his now-classic *American Catholics and the Intellectual Life* with this quote from the British historian D. W. Brogan: "In no western society is the intellectual prestige of Catholicism lower than in the country where, in such respects as wealth, numbers, and strength of organization, it is so powerful." Ellis generally agreed with Brogan's assessment. Looking back at the history of the church in the U.S., Ellis identified four factors explaining the dearth of Catholic intellectuals.

1. A ghetto mentality, developed in reaction to anti-Catholicism but in large part self-imposed, kept Catholics out of the intellectual mainstream.

2. The need for the church to absorb wave after wave of immigrants kept Catholics in a kind of chronic deficit with respect to anything other than bread-and-butter issues.

3. A Eurocentric view of the church's intellectual life seemed to suffice for American Catholics.

4. The lack of wealth—today we might say surplus wealth— kept Catholics from sufficiently supporting and endowing institutions of higher learning: universities, libraries, research centers, fellowships. Magazines!

Ellis' essay was followed in 1958 by Thomas O'Dea's *American Catholic Dilemma: An Inquiry into the Intellectual Life* in which O'Dea supplemented Ellis' historical survey with a sociological analysis. O'Dea looked at the conditions that not only produced so few intellectuals among American Catholics, but also engendered a kind of anti-intellectualism in the very settings where Catholic intellectuals should otherwise have been thriving—Catholic colleges and universities. In his view it was the deeply embedded attitudes of U.S. Catholics and the maintenance of those attitudes in seminaries, colleges, and universities that kept Catholics from making an intellectual contribution to their church and their society. He described five.

1. Intellectual formalism in which demonstrations replaced search, abstractions replaced experience, formulae replaced content, and rationalistic elaboration replaced genuine ontological insight. This tendency of Catholics to see the world as "finished" had its impact on attitudes toward science, philosophy, and the social sciences.

2. Authoritarianism—the tendency of ecclesiastical authorities to impose solutions or resolve conflicts by the pronouncement of formal statements—a situation about which O'Dea observed that the tension between the Catholic scholar and the Catholic community is reduced to that between the mischief-maker and the policeman.

3. Clericalism—to see and respond to all problems, tasks, risks, and achievements from a clerical point of view, that is, "from the professional perspective of the priest as an ecclesiastical official."

4. Moralism—the tendency to see the world as a place of moral danger to the Christian, a possible occasion of sin; in shunning worldly dangers a kind of moralism developed that was legalistic or ethically formalistic. As O'Dea noted, this placed the laity and the lay vocation in a precarious and always problematic position vis-à-vis the church and the clergy. It cast a shadow over the primary arena of lay concerns and lay activity.

5. Defensiveness: a long history of minority status, discrimination, prejudice, and even persecution tended to produce rigidity and a strongly felt need to repulse attack, real or imagined. It also, in O'Dea's view, kept us from examining our own condition in a frank and calm manner. It was very difficult for us to see and understand those in-built tendencies to formalism, authoritarianism, clericalism, and moralism that kept us from participating in American intellectual life.

O'Dea saw these five characteristics as having both latent and manifest expressions in the Catholic worldview, in teaching, in argumentation, in the formation of priests and religious women. Particularly in their latent form they helped to explain what Ellis' history could not account for—the persistence of an anti-intellectual outlook even given the altered circumstances American Catholics faced following World War II: mass immigration had ended in the twenties, Catholics were beginning to achieve middle-class status on a broad scale, higher education was increasingly open to and available for Catholics, and there was greater acceptance of Catholics by the general culture.

In retrospect we see an important and unvoiced question in this debate—the question of whether Americans generally shared an animus against intellectuals, or, more accurately, a vast indifference to them. Americans are a pragmatic and political people, more interested in doing than in thinking about what we are doing, more interested in behavior than in ideas.

Those factors in our specifically Catholic history and those features of our Catholic mental outlook that O'Dea and Ellis pointed to were important definers of Catholic culture, but they existed in a larger cultural context that was itself anti-intellectual.

The third book I want to talk about, therefore, is Richard Hofstatder's *Anti-Intellectualism in American Life.* Published in 1962, it focused on the larger culture's resistance and reaction to modernity expressed in three strands of the American character, one of them being the persistent anti-intellectualism of evangelical Protestantism. This Hofstatder saw as coming down on one side of a perennial strain in Christianity itself, that is, the tension between reason and emotion in legitimating religious belief. Did one know salvation, or feel it? Hofstatder related his thesis about evangelical Protestants to Catholics; he accepted John Tracy Ellis' outlook and conclusions and meshed them with his own theme—that the anti-intellectual impulse in American culture sprang to a great extent, not simply from an anti-intellectual tendency in Protestant fundamentalism but, in addition, from its resistance to and its revolt against modernity, the realm par excellence of the intellectuals. While denying any fundamentalist affinity, many Catholics would have happily agreed to the revolt against modernity. Certainly the linkages that Hofstadter drew among religion, resistance to modernity, and anti-intellectualism are there, and they are linkages not untypical of a certain Catholic outlook.

But in the subtext of his book, Hofstadter also voiced a persistent view among secularized Americans that religion and the intellectual life were necessarily at odds, at least as Hofstadter, a secular Jew, understood the nature of intellectual life and religious belief. Ellis and O'Dea, of course, thought no such thing. The puzzle for them was why a church with so rich an intellectual tradition had not produced its share of intellectuals in a land where resources and opportunities were so abundant, and where, so they believed, a rich intellectual life flourished in quarters other than the Catholic community.

Were they right?

First experience: At the time Ellis and O'Dea were writing, I was a student in high school. Had I known of their criticisms, I would have said, "You're wrong." That's how I talked in high school! I would have named some among my teachers who were bright and imaginative; I would have argued that the curriculum was exposing me and my fellow students to the moral questions, political quandaries, the big questions, in ways that would engage us in the world of ideas and their political and moral consequences. I might have said this out of naiveté, perhaps out of an unguarded enthusiasm. But perhaps I was having a different experience. I thought I was being introduced to the world of ideas. Furthermore, I was growing up in Chicago (which is a place different from New York and Washington, where O'Dea and Ellis wrote). I was growing up in the 1950s—a time of great change for Catholics. And I was growing up in a Catholic subculture that was confident and competent. I would have contested the bleakness of the picture they drew.

In college I might have hesitated, and I would have been more astute in recognizing some of the character deforming qualities that O'Dea, in particular, identified. But I didn't leave that Catholic high school in 1959, or my Catholic university in 1963, unprepared to deal with many of the issues that perplex us today, from bioethics to the bomb, from housing questions to race, from an understanding of the holocaust to the wakening realization that the church had been, and still was, plagued by serious and compromising church/ state questions in Spain, Germany, Italy, and Austria. So in the end I would have not so much denied Ellis' and O'Dea's points as argued that things have changed and are changing.

A new era was dawning in American Catholic life. John Kennedy was the most conspicuous and public symbol of Catholic assimilation into the mainstream of American life, with all of the advantages and drawbacks that that brought with it. Kennedy represented no challenge to the prevailing separation of church and state, nor to the separation of church and culture. His form of Catholicism accommodated easily to the confident, expansionist, and innocent America of the early 1960s. Americans had answers —or so we thought—to many of the world's problems, and so did Catholics. Kennedy was even reported to have an intellectual bent —a kind of pragmatic, problem-solving intellect, attitude. Furthermore, here was a lay Catholic exercising the ultimate responsibilities of an American; it was an important model of leadership and independence to which many Catholics, young and old, responded in a positive way. The worldly tasks of governing, organizing, problem-solving achieved a kind of worthiness they had lacked in a church seen to be clerical, hierarchical, otherworldly, inward turning.

The second experience I share with most of you: the 1960s. Change continued in the church and in American society. The revolution of John XXIII clearly summed up much work that had been done and set us forth on a new and sometimes rocky pilgrimage. American churchmen played an important role at the Second Vatican Council, and in some respects none more than John Courtney Murray, who respected both Catholic and American traditions and meshed them, to the advantage not only of Americans but of the world church and the world, period. The Declaration on Religious Liberty, along with the Constitutions on the Church and the Church in the Modern World, presented Catholics, and U.S. Catholics in particular, with a new set of ideas and a new outlook about the work of the Christian in the world.

A quarter-century later, we live in a very different world and a very different church. America is no longer so confident of its goodness or its benign intentions, of its economic competence or its military power. Some have described a loss of innocence. Yet we remain a rich and powerful country. As part of the mainstream, Catholics benefit from that wealth and bear responsibility for the use of that power. The church too has suffered a certain loss of innocence, a deep questioning of purpose and practice, a certain hesitation in coming to terms with our place in American culture.

Nonetheless, in so many ways, it seems to me, the U.S. Catholic church has come through the 1960s and 1970s in a sounder and sturdier condition than has American culture, which seems adrift and floundering, not sure what questions must be asked in order to find our bearings. The absence of a credible and serious public conversation about this loss of purpose drives people to the individualism, consumerism, and technological fixes so characteristic of the American response to crisis. In contrast, U.S. Catholics have much to offer. We are ready, it would seem, to take up the tasks of being American, being Catholic, being intellectuals.

For that too has changed. There are Catholics who are intellectuals. Ellis was looking for Catholic intellectuals as scholars and academics distinguished in their fields and acclaimed so by the larger discipline. Such men and women work in your institutions;

so do accomplished Catholic scholars in secular institutions. Ellis also pointed to the lack of first-rate American theologians. This too has changed. There are distinguished American theologians, scripture scholars, canonists, ecclesiologists engaged in a conversation that responds to the questions at the edge of belief and doubt, church men and women concerned about the credibility of religious thought and Catholic teaching—more so, it often appears, than the Congregation for the Doctrine of the Faith: the latest twist in the Curran case inevitably raises the question of whether Rome fully grasps that in an effort to assert and maintain authority they foolishly squander it.

Second, O'Dea defined intellectuals somewhat more broadly than Ellis, as "those men and women whose main interest is the advancement of knowledge, or the clarification of cultural issues and public problems." Here too Catholics have moved in: politicians; jurists; writers and political analysts; novelists, essayists, and artists.

Third: and there are those who do not speak to either a national or a disciplinary audience, those whom I earlier called local intellectuals; men and women who take ideas—ideas of all kinds—seriously and are ready and able to share, to argue, to carry on an unending conversation with one another, with students, and with the community. Certainly such intellectuals exist in your schools. They may be teachers, they may be scholars, deans, even presidents.

There are intellectuals all right. Yet as you focus on your agenda for the U.S. Catholic intellectual community, you will probably stop, as we often do at *Commonweal* editorial meetings, and ask: Where are the Catholic intellectuals? Where is the community of thinkers able to speak, write, argue about our issues?

We have some names and addresses. Yet, for a community of fifty-two million Catholics, our list is short. There are not enough of us, a critical mass, so to speak, of Catholic intellectuals—not simply a Catholic who happens to be an intellectual or an intellectual who happens to be a Catholic. But a Catholic intellectual. And here let me return for a moment to the question of definition.

Ellis and O'Dea assumed that if a Catholic managed to become an intellectual there would be no problem in being a Catholic intellectual because Catholic identity was so pronounced. We have breached the ghetto walls, the ghetto mindset, and the ghetto behavior patterns. Many Catholics have achieved first-rank status as scholars, physicians, lawyers, novelists, playwrights, politicians, public servants, and among these are some first-rate intellectuals. But what they have become is Americans.

Ellis and O'Dea overlooked three problems. First, they overestimated the strength of Catholic structures, organization, and identity. Second, they did not notice the indifference to ideas and to intellectuals in the larger culture—an indifference, even hostility, paralleled by the church's own deeply ambivalent attitude toward intellectuals. Third, they did not understand the tendency in U.S. culture to privatize religion and religious thought—so if you're a Catholic anything, or a Mormon anything, or a Plymouth Brethren anything, it is the anything-but-religion that the larger culture will find interesting about you.

The bottom line on numbers comes up low because there are few models of the Catholic intellectual for younger Catholics to follow; because for different reasons neither the church nor American culture particularly values intellectuals whose religious outlook shapes their ideas, so that there are few institutional supports for their work; and finally because, though we have not purged all the old forms of anti-intellectualism, there are some new ones to tempt us. Three temptations.

1. Prophetic anti-intellectualism. Prophets see no real need for intellectual search. The real problems of American culture and Catholic culture are clear; and so are the answers. What is needed to change things are not ideas but an act of will, courage, and the appropriation of gospel values. The prophet is impatient with discussion, with negotiation, with compromise, with history, with analysis, even with criticism other than the criticism of the prophetic judgment. There are prophets of the left and right. Some hammer away on missiles. Some burn abortion clinics. Some give themselves over to the latest revolution. The idea that real change comes with persuasion, education, changed conviction, that real change is complex and long-term, is, in the mind of the prophet, one of the delusions of Catholic intellectuals. This is often an attractive model for young Catholics who find in prophetic certainty a welcome relief from middle-class complacency, but also from the

complexities and ambiguities of twentieth century church culture and American culture.

2. Psychological anti-intellectualism: we see this in the new spiritualities that preach the cultivation of the heart and the emotions as the seat of understanding and conversion. This reaction to past formalism, rationalism, and moralism ends in minimizing, even dismissing, reason and intellect as essential components of Catholic theology and religious belief. Faith and feeling displace the traditional links between faith and reason not only in favor of various forms of pietism, quietism, and privatism, but also of certain kinds of enthusiasms and do-goodism. Robert Bellah and his colleagues have shown in *Habits of the Heart* how congenial a form of religion this is for Protestant Americans; it has its growing Catholic counterpart.

3. Inconoclastic anti-intellectualism: much secular culture does exhibit an unfortunate dogmatism, including liberal sectors, that traditionally pride themselves on being non-dogmatic. Today we see new iconoclasts, religious iconoclasts scoring points off this secular dogmatism, shrewdly stealing modernism's thunder by casting themselves in the roles of brave dissenters against the conformism of others. The new iconoclasm may seem exhilarating, especially to its practitioners, but this is psychological warfare, not argument. Their smugness feeds off of an existing one. If the standby attitudes of modern secularism are worn thin, that does not necessarily pump blood back into the inherited attitudes of traditional religion. It is possible that both are wanting. And only careful inquiry and argument can decide the issues.

In these new forms of anti-intellectualism and in lingering examples of the old, we continue to see among liberals and conservatives, radicals and reactionaries, various aspects of authoritarianism, formalism, moralism, and defensiveness that on the one hand deform Catholic intellectual life, and, on the other, turn away and defeat Catholics and intellectuals who would like to carry on the conversations that link their work and their faith, their life and their church.

I did caution you at the beginning that this was often a disheartening conversation. What is to be done?

Commonweal is a very small institution; yet as its editor I share with you, who edit much larger institutions, certain assumptions: 1. ideas count; 2. being Catholic counts; 3. the way we shape our ideas, connect and disconnect them from one another, reject and accept them, are deeply tied, are central to the story we tell ourselves about what it means to be an American Catholic.

To do that seriously there are three factors we need to work at: identity, rigor, respect.

1. Identity: are we Catholic or not? When we call ourselves a Catholic magazine, or Catholic college, or Catholic university, what do we mean. In name only? There has been a tendency to abandon identity, to secularize institutions in structure and often in practice. Every time a staff opening is announced at *Commonweal,* the magazine has been approached by people, Catholic and non-Catholic, who think an explicitly Catholic journal is out of date. I am sure you have had the same discussions. This tendency to deny or downplay Catholic identity has an equally unfortunate counter-tendency in the assertion of Catholic identity by reverting to a vicious cycle of authoritarianism as the trustees of Catholic University are doing or by insisting that Catholic identity consists in a blind identification with what some conservative groups call papal orthodoxy.

The appalling spectacle of one of our most scrupulous, thoughtful, and quintessentially Catholic moral thologians being hounded out of the country's flagship Catholic university is all too apt to provoke the unfortunate reaction, "If this is Catholic identity, who needs it?" Cardinal Ratzinger has encouraged us to reaffirm an age-old belief in the devil. I can't help wondering, at the very moment of a new sensitivity to Catholic identity in the church's institutions of higher learning, what imp it was that sent the Congregation for the Doctrine of the Faith on such a self-destructive course of action.

Where does identity come from?

Our identity lies in a long Catholic tradition, in the particular history of our institution, and in our response to present conditions. When I became editor of *Commonweal* this past January, I went to a magazine that has a sixty-five year tradition of being a journal of public affairs, religion, literature, and the arts edited by Roman Catholic laypeople. In continuing that tradition I have a two-part task: first to honestly try to understand the facts of the matter, be they third world debt, the pope's newest encyclical, or public education; second, to draw on *Commonweal's* Catholic tradition and our own understanding of Catholicism to frame and interpret those facts. *Commonweal* has been a bridge for a two-way conversation between faith and life; my job is to continue that conversation. We are a particular tradition operating in the framework of the Catholic one. Though non-Catholics write in our pages, in a straightforward and unembarrassed way we have to be clear about our own identity in commissioning manuscripts, reviews, opinion pieces, and sometimes in rejecting them. We have to be that in our own writing and editing. Each of you has such a tradition to draw on from your own history as well as from our common tradition. If we have worked carefully to delineate our Catholic identity, then there are some ways that we will find ourselves at odds with our culture, while in others we will be deeply in tune with it.

I have never been the president of a Catholic university, nor have I ever taught in one. But I was a student in one. And I think I know what in my university education kept me Catholic: intellectual substance and a sufficient number of adults who considered themselves Catholic intellectuals. In detail this meant a theology course every semester, only half of which were any good; a philosophy course every semester—all of which were splendid except for two ethics courses, and something called rational psychology; a liberal arts curriculum that taught me to think, to write, to understand some of the achievements of western culture as well as many of its worst mistakes. I was taught by men and women who took ideas seriously and thought I should too (the local intellectuals). I had friends who practiced at being poets, short story writers, philosophers, politicians, philosopher kings—fellow students who thought at least their ideas mattered. And then there was the usual bureaucratic nuttiness and institutional injustices that spurred us all to political action. Being Catholic and being intellectual was hard work, but it was never seen, by my best teachers and my best friends, as anything other than totally possible and totally absorbing. Here was a Catholic community that took ideas seriously.

2. Rigor: if you're clear about the Catholic identity of your institution, it's easier to tell what fits and what doesn't; what will

work and what won't; what's probably true and what's probably false; what's a good idea and what's a crummy one. But still, identity does not absolve us from being critical, from delineating criteria and applying them. *Commonweal* editors read hundreds of manuscripts a year. That we agree on rejecting so many and accepting so few means we share a standard about what fits the magazine's tradition as well as a standard about what is intelligent, helpful, informative, moving writing, and what is not. We look for honesty and clarity of expression. We distinguish moralizing from moral analysis; church talk and liberal cant from real language; empty phrases from ones filled with meaning. As you who read the magazine know, sometimes we fail. Why? I suppose because we let our good intentions get in the way of our better judgments; or we aren't as critical as we should be of people on the right side of an issue with a bad argument. Rigor means saying no to friends.

I point to my own work because I imagine in some ways it is like your own process of interviewing and selecting faculty, of reforming curricula, of admitting students, of putting together lecture programs. Your work requires similar efforts in examining, judging, and choosing. Being a Catholic college or university, as our being a Catholic magazine, requires a respect for the person or the object of our scrutiny, the ability to know whether he, she, or it fits, and the ability to say either yes or no for sound reasons.

3. So I've said be Catholic—if that's what you are; be smart, be rigorous in maintaining that identity; and finally be respectful. I use the word "respect" for want of a better word, and I mean a number of things by it. If we think we are doing important work, if we respect our institutions and traditions, and the people with whom we work, then we need to give them what Iris Murdoch calls a patient, loving regard; we need to pay attention to them. And it is hard to pay attention, often because we think Catholic institutions and Catholic intellectuals and Catholic anything are not quite first rate. We are too proud to say we're only second-rate . . . but we do say things like—if only we had better students, if only the English department published more, if only *Commonweal* could afford better paper. Well, yes, yes, and yes. But it distracts us—it distracts us from turning a patient, loving regard on what we do have, of using it and building it up. And in that vein, I return to the local intellec-

tuals, the college within the college, the community of scholars and teachers who value ideas, who pass them on, who test them. They are essential to the vitality of your institution, this church, and this culture.

Turn a patient, loving regard on yourselves, on your institutions, on your local intellectuals.

See yourselves for what you are, Catholic colleges and universities that are a public resource, critical to the task of carrying on a coherent conversation about church and world, faith and life, ethics and the workplace; of establishing the links between knowledge and justice; of helping your own students, your faculty, trustees, the parents of your students, the members of your communities, to make sense out of what is a fragmented culture. American culture is desperate for a conversation about public issues set in a moral framework: whether that issue is public education, foreign policy, or third world debt. Our culture needs an effective and credible moral critique of consumerism, militarism, racism, and technological fixes. The university is able to draw in many who are not part of your community. Encourage that conversation, build a sense of community that flows from your practice and your conviction that Catholics and ideas are not a contradiction in terms.

American culture has reached the limits of the enlightenment paradigm; we live with a sense that progress, technology, the utilitarian can-do spirit all have their limits, and we have reached them, or we are almost there. Human nature, nature herself, history and tradition, basic human needs for community, continuity, and solidarity simply cannot be set aside or "transcended" in the creation of a paradise on earth.

It is no great surprise that everyone's favorite institution for solving these problems, an institution that has never burned a bridge behind it, should be the one, the only, the Catholic Church. We hear much of the Catholic moment. But it is a moment in which many are competing to write our agenda—some who want us to be the source of social discipline and order, some who want us to pump energy and effort into revolutionary movements, some who want us to pick up where the Protestants have fallen off—to become the civil religion. We need to write the agenda for ourselves.

American Culture as a Challenge
to Catholic Intellectuals

John A. Coleman, S.J.

> th' first thing ye know there won't be as many pages iv'
> advertisin' as there are iv' lithrochoor. Then people will
> stop readin' magazines. A man don't want to dodge
> around through almost impenetrable pomes an' reform
> articles to find a pair iv' suspenders or shavin' soap.[1]
>
> FINLEY PETER DUNNE, "MR. DOOLEY ON THE
> MAGAZINES" (1909)

Mr. Dooley, perusing the magazines at the turn of this century, knew intuitively that what they proclaimed in their layouts signified that, as a later president, Calvin Coolidge, would solemnly declare: "The business of America is business." A century earlier, that astute viewer of American mores, Alexis de Tocqueville, saw the United States as the prime exemplar of a commercial democracy: a business civilization.

I want to highlight in this essay three salient themes of this American commercial democracy as challenges to Catholic intellectual life: consumerism, technology and individualism. The last of these themes is as old in American culture as the nation itself. Tocqueville coined the term "individualism" to capture the peculiar genius of the new mercantile democracy. An American romance with technology, in its turn, starts as far back as Thomas Jefferson's and Ben Franklin's enlightenment hopes which rested on a belief in the liberating spirit of innovative technology. Indeed one of the most astute cultural analyses of American society and culture, authored by Leo Marx, teases out the dialectic of technology and the land in its title, *The Machine in the Garden.*[1]

37

While consumerism as a full-blown cultural phenomenon in America occurs only after the gilded age (circa 1880), very early on—even in Puritan times, as David Shi has argued—the dream of America as a garden of affluence undermined the alternative religious and early republican ideal of plain living and the simple life.[2] In a sense, consumerism lies already ingredient in the early overemphasis in America on freedom of choice, a peculiarly voluntaristic valuation of freedom as *simple* choice—sacred *because* of the choosing—aptly captured in the most American Sun Oil advertisement in the early post-war period which announced, "There is only one freedom, freedom of choice."[3]

SEEING AMERICA AS ONE CULTURE

Before we take up consumerism, technology and individualism as cultural challenges to American intellectual life, however, we will need to fasten onto a working definition of culture, at least for the purposes of this essay. As many commentators from the arena of the social sciences, especially anthropology, note, the affirmation of a unitary culture in advanced technological societies presents serious conceptual problems. These voices contest the Durkheimian consensus view of culture as inappropriate for anything but simpler societies and propose, in its stead, radical cultural pluralism. They see in modern societies competing and sharply contested ideals of the good life shaped by divergent social classes, geographic regions, ethnic and religious groups and intellectual traditions. Rather than a zone of cultural consensus, this position proposes a view of modern society as a combat zone.

A culture—if there is such a thing—can be usefully defined as a "relatively" integrated set of *creed, cult* and *code* (note the tentativeness about the postulated integration). If there should be such a thing as a culture, however, it would remain a somewhat ambiguous text, subject to some contestation. Does America possess a "relatively" integrated set of creed, cult and code which functions as a "somewhat" stable—if contested—cultural text? I would submit the answer is yes.

CULTURE AS CREED

Hervé Verenne, a French emigré anthropologist who has wrestled with the issue of symbolizing America as one culturally, notes certain dominant themes usually associated with America: individualism, choice, progress through machines, the state and the corporation.[4] Other commentators stress, with Tocqueville, the notions of democracy and an almost promiscuous public friendliness. Still others follow Tocqueville's stress on the paradoxical marriage in America of independence (the "self-reliant" individual) and conformity—the simultaneous American desire to be integrated with the group and to be unique. Finally, several cultural commentators stress the newly emergent "therapeutic ethic" as dominant in American life.[5] All of these attempts try to picture culture as a creed: a set of beliefs about human nature, action and purpose.

Two auxiliary notions will be absolutely necessary to conceive of America as, in some sense, one culture in creed: the concept of hegemony (borrowed from Antonio Gramsci) and the concept of a hierarchy of values where certain values form a defining stamp to the set, subsuming other values under their mantle.

HEGEMONY

T. J. Jackson Lears speaks to the Gramscian notion of cultural hegemony:

> The Italian Marxist Antonio Gramsci used the concept of cultural hegemony to suggest that ruling groups dominate a society not merely through brute force but also through intellectual and moral leadership. In other words, a ruling class needs more than businessmen, soldiers and statesmen; it also requires publicists, professors, ministers and literati who help to establish the society's conventional wisdom—the boundaries of permissible debate about human nature and the social order. Outside these boundaries, opinions can be labeled "tasteless", "irresponsible" and in general unworthy of serious consideration. Even if ordinary people do not consciously embrace the conventional wisdom, it shapes their tacit assumptions in subtle ways. . . . By helping to create a taken-for-granted "reality," the leaders of the dominant culture identify beliefs that are in the interest of a particular class with the "na-

tional" common sense of society (and indeed of humanity) at large.
Yet cultural hegemony is not maintained mechanistically or conspiratorially. A dominant culture is not a static superstructure but a continual process. . . . The changes in the dominant culture are not always deliberately engineered; at times they stem from attempts to resolve private dilemmas that seem to have little to do with the public realm of class domination. Without conspiring to do so, sometimes with wholly other ends in view, the ruling groups continually refashion the prevailing structure of feeling to express—more or less—their own changing experience.[6]

If we pay attention to the realities of class and power in society, it will be permissible to speak of a dominant or hegemonic creed with which contesting parties to the creed must come to grips. It—rather than the contesters—defines the cultural terms of the debate. Note too that intellectuals play a determinative role in supporting the culturally defined sense of the real. One thinks here of Theodore Roosevelt's remark to a political adversary that "we do not have classes at all on this side of the Atlantic"—a piece of conventional wisdom that has widely shaped American opinion throughout the twentieth century, particularly strengthened in the post-war period by "the end of ideology" theorists in the social sciences and the American-exception school of historians. Culture and social reality may not be static. There occurs an ongoing social construction of reality. Still, some dominant themes (and interests) remain relatively stable in American life. Clearly, the values of consumerism (affluence through goods), technology as liberating promise and pattern for understanding life and individualism constitute, arguably, the most salient of these themes. Moreover, as we will see, they reinforce one another. Consumerism promotes individualist patterns; the liberating promise of technology is tied to its role in increasing consumer goods.

VALUE HIERARCHY

The second needed clarification comes from the earlier anthropological work of Clyde Kluckhohn and associates who argued that cultures, typically, constitute a hierarchy of values.[7] It may be less helpful, in cross-cultural comparisons, to seek out total contrasts on cultural values, as if value x were simply absent in one culture and value y in another. Rather cultures represent hierarchical sets where certain values—e.g. individualistic freedom in the American case—subordinate (but do not entirely eclipse) alternative and corollary values, e.g. solidarity.

In this way of thinking, Indian society also includes some form of individual choice as a cultural value but subordinated to communal solidarities while in the United States an opposing hierarchy obtains. Those who especially emphasize communal solidarities in the United States (as opposed to individualism) or simple living (as opposed to consumerism) and focal practices (as opposed to the devise paradigm in technology) are constrained to stake out their opposition to a hegemonic value hierarchy where consumerism, individualism and technology define the cultural argument. The other values are recognized but only as subordinate elements.

In some sense, counter-cultural proposals in America which do not do justice to the claims of consumerism, individualism and the technical paradigm will be ruled out of court as heretical to the American creed. One of the ironies, indeed, of the counter-cultural movements of the 1960s consists in the extensive way in which they embodied in their slogans ("Do your own thing") and actions the epitome of American individualism. They incarnated an old American individualist theme of "picking up roots" and starting over. Their counter-cultural style (levis, rock music, new age diet) became marketed as hot consumer items. As a final irony, these counter-cultural baby boomers have undergone metamorphosis to become the yuppie advocates of the new technology of Silicon Valley in the 1980s.[8] Settled cultural creeds seeped into—"infected"— their desire to be counter-cultural.

CULTURE AS CULT

In a somewhat moralistic, if useful, book, *Following Christ in a Consumer Society,* John Kavanaugh proposes the notion of a culture as a cult: "A culture is a cult . . . it is a revelation system. . . . It quietly converts, elicits commitments, transforms, provides heroes, suggests human fulfillments. The culture, then, is a gospel—a book of revelation—mediating beliefs, revealing us to ourselves . . . a culture is a cultivation."[9]

A culture constitutes a cultivation, especially, of representative types. Robert Bellah and his associates in their much acclaimed study *Habits of the Heart* refer to three main American representative character types: the entrepreneur (now being surpassed), the manager and the therapist. Cultures cultivate specific types of humanity. In America, the manager-type reinforces technical rationality and the therapist-type applauds hedonistic consumerism and defines all problems in individualistic psychological terms. The permutations of these three inter-related themes of consumerism, technology and individualism are both subtle and hydra-headed.

But there exist, for Kavanaugh, false cults and cultures:

> A spiritual and psychic problem emerges when the culture, which is *a part* of the human, achieves an independence from living, producing humans, expresses only one part of the wholly human, and dominates the humans who produce it. People serve culture. Culture no longer serves them. . . . As alienation, culture is a frozen artifact against which the newness of human imagination is rigidly measured and against which the persistent human hopes for fulfillments, rights and values are dashed. It is an estranged house—protecting not persons, but fragmentary forms of human life. In this sense, culture does not teach, it propagandizes. It is not a sacred expression of the human. It is an idolatry—in whose fabricated image humans are recreated and diminished.[10]

We must ask, then, about culture as cultivation and cult, how this culture liberates, engages and actualizes our faith. Here we are asking about serious inculturation. "But we must also ask ourselves: how does culture threaten, confine, compromise and betray our faith? This is the question we most frequently forget."[11] Here we pose the counter-cultural claims of the faith which states that it stands above every culture.

CULTURE AS CODE

Culture is likewise—and primarily—a codified set of constraints and expectations: a code. Culture is a system of signals for behavior and action, signals which promise the sanction of reward and/or disapproval. Hervé Verenne is especially helpful in conceptualizing culture as a code or constraining pattern. Verenne stresses that the anthropologist should place emphasis less on elucidating some elusive "American mind" or character than on "whatever one can not escape in the United States."[12] In this regard, Verenne notes the pervasive remarks of the foreign visitors about American public friendliness. Even adversaries in America display friendliness to one another in public. Are Americans really more friendly than other peoples? Verenne does not venture as much nor think it a good question. Rather, "friendliness is above all a problem that all those who live in the United States have to deal with."[13]

Problems that all those who live in a culture have to deal with! Here we see the meaning of culture as a code. Culture is not a statistical congeries of psychological properties. At heart, it is not, per se, statistical at all. Rather, "America is a gloss for a particular patterning or structure. It is not an object nor is it a population." It is a code of constraints and expectations, a symbolic network that all those who live in America have to deal with.[14]

AN AMBIGUOUS TEXT

Finally, any culture is an ambiguous text. Any living culture represents a lively argument about the goods and goals of a tradition. All classics—and *a fortiori* the classic persons, founding events and texts of a given culture—have supercharged and historically contested meanings (if not in the interpretation of their origins then in the interpretation of their contemporary relevance). Like the interpretation of any text, our reading of culture must be critical. In an essay entitled "On the Anthropology of America," John Caughey signals this critical function of deciphering culture: "If our culture is a 'text', then we should seek to understand its structure in order to identify its strengths—with an eye to consolidating them —and to identify its flaws, with an eye toward alleviating them."[15]

I have suggested that John Kavanaugh's reading of American consumerism verges toward a moralism. A moralistic reading of cultural traits all too often stakes out easy contrasts between good points and bad points in a culture as if one could rather handily have one without the other, to separate the wheat from the chaff, the sheep from the goats. A moralistic reading sharply and too simply proposes counter-culture to cultural text as if (1) the cultural text could be easily supplanted, and (2) the counter-cultural movement could remain untainted by dominant and pervasive cultural themes.

A much wiser approach to the issues of cultural discernment can be found in Tocqueville's classic study of early American democracy. The aristocratic Tocqueville, neither a stouthearted nor unnuanced friend of democracy, saw the cultural weight—and almost historical inevitability—of emergent democracy in the early nineteenth century. He notes its perils of mass conformity, the leveling of tastes and standards of excellence, its classical temptation to avarice and the unchained pursuit of wealth, its insidious temptations to "soft" despotism. Yet Tocqueville proposed no conscious contrasting counter-culture, no new form of the aristocratic principle he preferred, since he yielded the constraining force of the new cultural ideal, interests and emerging institutions. His advice to his contemporaries in France was to go into the almost inevitable new patterns with eyes wide open to their dangers and seductions and to work patiently to coax out their strengths and temper their deformations. Tocqueville proposed a reform of the paradigm from within it by taming its excesses and correcting, where possible, for its imbalances. He despaired of simply rejecting what seemed to him, in any event, culturally inevitable. Yet he did not merely acquiesce in the emerging cultural form.

Robert Bellah et al. in *Habits of the Heart* rather similarly sketch an individualism and a therapeutic ethos out of control. Yet they do not succumb to a moralistic proposal to replace American individualism and the therapeutic ethos with some purely counter-cultural communitarianism. They do not abandon either the enlightenment or the bourgeois individualistic revolution. Nor do they seek to engraft a foreign shoot on the American tree. They pointedly cite the many accomplishments of individualism and therapy and champion their values. They lodge their complaint primarily against the near total eclipse of older American languages of culture and the over-extension of the therapeutic and individual-istic models. They attempt to channel these two to their proper, delimited spheres.

So, too, the best cultural critics of the technological paradigm —one thinks of Lewis Mumford's classic critique and the recent brilliant study of Albert Borgmann, *Technology and the Character of Contemporary Life*—approach the excesses of the technological paradigm by a strategy of recognition and restraint. The recognition notes the pervasiveness of what Borgmann calls "the devise para-digm," its oppressive reduction of most of life to "how-to" issues, its conflation of all areas of life to technical "problems" rather than "mystery."[16]

Tocqueville, Bellah, Borgmann avoid an a-cultural either/or rejection of pervasive cultural elements (even deeply tainted cul-tural elements such as consumerism). Thus, too, Lewis Mumford takes pains in his *The Conduct of Life* to note, "It is not enough to say, as Rousseau once did, that one has only to reverse all the current practices to be right. If our new philosophy is well-grounded we shall not merely react against the 'air-conditioned nightmare' of our present culture; we shall also carry into the future many ele-ments of quality that this culture also embraces."[17] More to the point, any strategy of simply reversing current practices will be doomed to failure. Precisely as a-cultural, it represents a moralism.

Too often, unfortunately, the Catholic intellectual critiques of culture have, as in Kavanaugh's study of consumerism, verged to-ward moralism. Their virtue has been that they see the moral issues, even dangers, in cultural trends. But as a species of moralism, they forego the first stage of recognition which asks "Why is this cultural element so salient?" and whether it is deeply rooted in social insti-tutions and symbol, perhaps ineradicably so. Moralisms refuse the ascesis, proper to the intellectual life, of stepping back—as a meth-odological moment—from the moral focus to pursue an analytic recognition of, for example, why the sexual revolution or competi-tive consumerism has such deep tendrils in modern cultural soil. Even the much and properly praised bishops' pastoral on the econ-omy may fall into this kind of moralism devoid of a deeper cultural recognition of the roots of competitive capitalism in institutions and culturally cultivated character structures. This represents, at least, the penetrating if almost sympathetic critique of the pastoral letter by Norman Birnbaum.[18]

Secondly, too often these moralistic critiques follow a strategy of rejection or sheer counter-cultural substitution. Besides being naive, in an anthropological sense, these moralistic approaches neglect the very patient discernment models of culture inherent in the gospel's parable of the wheat and the chaff and its lovely metaphor of faith and discipleship as leavening presence within culture. Analytic recognition of a cultural code of restrictions and expectations leads to the corollary attitude of restraint: coaxing strengths, tolerating some lesser evils, tethering worst case scenarios and tendencies, tilting against imbalances. Cultures are never infinitely malleable. Put bluntly, to take away American individualism, consumerism and the technological paradigm would remove the very skeleton from the American body. For all the unlovely features of that body, it remains the contours of ours as Americans and American Catholic intellectuals.

In the end, however, a consistent strategy of recognition (eyes wide open to the ideological features of cultural elements) and restraint (putting Pandora back in her rightful box; recognizing the legitimate claims but restraining their imperialistic impulses) represents a quite radical and even revolutionary proposal in American intellectual life. It typifies neither our ordinary intellectual institutions nor churches or media. Few indeed recognize the costs and pervasiveness, the hidden agendas and consequences of consumerism, technology and individualism as elements of American culture.

It will be my simple contention that a deep historical understanding (recognition) of these three pervasive American values and a moral intent to restrain their dominance *over* (indeed, submersion and near destruction *of*) other important values should be the goal of cultural literacy in our American Catholic universities. Yet these institutions themselves, all too often, have long mirrored rather than challenged a consumerist, technological and individualist view of education which is the regnant paradigm in American higher education. The tentacles of culture grasp widely.

I. CONSUMERISM:
THE AMERICAN GARDEN OF AFFLUENCE

At the turn of this century, the anti-establishment Chicago economist Thorstein Veblen, in his *Theory of the Leisure Class* (1899), already mocked American pecuniary emulation and conspicuous consumption. He saw America's culture of consumption as socially functional but morally bankrupt. Later, in their classic two sociological studies, *Middletown* (1929) and *Middletown in Transition* (1937), Robert and Helen Lynd defined America as, essentially, a consumer culture. They held Muncie, Indiana to be Veblen's pecuniary culture. What at the turn of the century had been true only of the rich now had spread to the middle classes. "The natives' belief and behavior in each sphere of life contributed to the maintenance of 'a culture where everything hinges on money'; that central focus itself conditioned future ideas and actions in a closed cycle of causation. The pecuniary culture that Veblen had detected thirty years before in the leisure class had now spread throughout the entire society. All of Muncie's primary rituals helped to buttress the reigning system of values."[19]

In more recent work, Richard Fox and Jackson Lears document the pervasiveness of consumer culture in the United States and try to discover the reason why consumption became a cultural ideal, a hegemonic "way of seeing" in twentieth century America.

Consumer culture is more than the 'leisure ethic' or the 'American standard of living'. It is an ethic, a standard of living and a power structure. Life for most middle-class and working-class Americans in the twentieth century has been a ceaseless pursuit of the 'good life' and a constant reminder of their powerlessness. Consumers are not only buyers of goods but recipients of professional advice, marketing strategies, government programs, electoral choices and advertisers' images of happiness. Although the dominant institutions of our culture have purported to be offering the consumer a fulfilling participation in the life of the community, they have to a large extent presented the empty prospect of taking part in the marketplace of personal exchange. Individuals have been invited to seek commodities as keys to personal welfare and even to conceive of their own selves as commodities. One sees not only one's labor and skills but one's image and personality, too. While the few make decisions about managing society, the many are left to manage their appearance, aided by trained counselors in personal cosmetics. Leadership by experts and pervasive self-absorption have developed symbiotically in American consumer culture. No doubt the spread of mass communication has lightened old burdens and brought genuine material improvements to the lives of many Americans. But the cost has been too high. People deserve a more democratic as well as a more affluent way of life.[20]

Far from being Marxists, Lears and Fox nevertheless see something like Marx's postulated commodity fetishism in American consumer society. An unconscious collaboration—a kind of Weberian "elective affinity"—tied the therapeutic ethos of consumerism to the interests of corporate proprietors and managers in the emerging consumer culture. Corporate advertising turned to the therapeutic ethic with its "promise that the product would contribute to the buyer's well-being and the threat that his well-being would be undermined if he failed to buy it."[21] Consumerist advertising embodies what the French sociologist Henri Lefebvre calls "the decline of the referentials," i.e. the tendency in corporate capitalism for words to become severed from any meaningful referent. Finally, notes Lears, "a quest for self-realization through consumption compensated for loss of autonomy on the job."[22]

What is a culture of consumerism? On what structural elements does it rest? What are its main cultural themes? How pervasive is it in America? Are there alternative cultural currents in American life to restrain it?

A CULTURE OF CONSUMERISM

Consumer culture represents a highly complex social construction. It is not well understood by the tendency among many commentators to moralize about it from an elitist perspective. We wrongly perceive the relationship of consumers to the producers if we assume that consumers have no control or are passive victims. Involvement in a consumer culture results from active choices and an active "buying into the project" by consumers. A consumer culture is neither imposed by conspiracy from above nor acquiesced in passively from below. Nor are consumer choices made totally irrationally as if the consumer were addicted to some drug. Consumption constitutes a social act structured by frameworks of meaning. People are "won over" to a consumer culture, not blinded and tricked into it.

People also draw from it selectively. They accept some aspects of it and reject others. Moreover, consumer culture is not the only culture from which people draw meaning for their lives. Indeed, consumer culture itself draws selectively from other cultural elements—from popular culture, youth culture, wider bourgeois culture. As an analytic element, however, consumer culture remains partially autonomous: it possesses its own themes, materials and mechanisms. We cannot totally reduce it to some other factor, even to corporate capitalism as such. For consumption is not a simple function of capital's need to reproduce itself. Nevertheless, a consumer culture can be defined as a way of life associated with and reproduced through the operations of consumer capitalism.

British sociologist John Hargreaves articulates for us the major themes of a culture of capitalism:

> It is the way other discourses and practices are articulated around the features of a consumer culture, and the way the whole complex is orchestrated by certain key themes, that gives it its coherence and power. The orchestrating themes of this culture are directed at selling a specifically modern pagan version of the good life. The dominant discourse/practice is of youth, beauty, romance, sexual attraction, energy, fitness, health, movement, excitement, adventure, freedom, exotica, luxury, enjoyment, entertainment, fun. Above all, this culture valorizes 'self-expression'. A truly astonishing variety of goods and services—from washing powder, cars and foreign holidays, to

cosmetics, fashion-wear, eating and aerobics circulate on this basis; and concomitantly, major segments of social life are organized around consumer culture.[23]

To nurture and sustain it, consumer culture relies on important structural elements in advanced capitalist society: the growing centralization of economic power among producers; the extended scale of bureaucratic control and market operations; the growing remoteness of controllers and decision-makers from local sites of decision; the packaging of family entertainment and sport.

Consumerism reinforces excessive individualism:

> What we encounter especially is a meticulous attention to those aspects of their lives that are deeply personal to people. The close attention to what is personally important can be seen in the way, for example, one's appearance (how one dresses, what cosmetics to use, whether one is too fat, how good one's teeth are), how one feels (headache? confident? happy?) and even how one smells are given priority. The discourse selects, from the range of experience, certain ways in which we are affected personally and offers personal solutions. Collective concerns and collective, as opposed to individual, forms of consumption as a solution to problems are largely absent from this discourse. The collective is displaced to the level of personal reality and the individual is made solely responsible for doing something about it. The priority given to individual autonomy and responsibility and the ideal of a private existence shows consumer culture drawing strongly on bourgeois tradition.[24]

That consumer culture has become pervasive in America is perhaps best caught in Daniel Boorstin's remark, "it would not be an overstatement to describe advertising as the characteristic rhetoric of democracy."[25] Moreover, we now speak of "selling" candidates to public office. As the journal *Nation's Business* proudly proclaimed already in 1956: "Both parties will merchandise their candidates and issues by the same methods that business has developed to sell goods."[26] In its turn, much of modern social science—especially sophisticated survey research—might aptly be dubbed the science of consumerism. The American fairy tale consists in two key premises: that more possessions mean more happiness and that a person who does or produces more is more important. The story of modernity is a tale of an inversion in priorities from a more ancient wisdom of the priority of persons over things to the modern paradigm of the priority of things over persons, indeed, the thingification of persons. This is what Marx meant when he evoked the phrase "commodity fetishism."

The dangers in this consumer culture—dangers both to the Christian faith and to our deeper humanity—are evoked by Kavanaugh: "We are only as we possess. We are what we possess. We are, consequently, possessed by our possessions, produced by our products."[27] Woe to the poor, handicapped, homely, elderly, shy and faltering in this world!

Yet Hargreaves reminds us wisely:

It is not that this kind of systematically produced imbalance displaces what is important with what is trivial; it is that this culture is hegemonized through the thematization of concerns which are, indeed, absolutely central to people's sense of identity, on the one hand, and the suppression of the relationship between these and other equally important public issues or collective concerns, on the other. For example, the discourse of diet gives priority to personal care of one's body but diet is not unrelated to the problem of food production, world prices and food shortages. Rather than express concern about the latter, consumer culture articulates diet with the issue of convenience foods and family life or *haute cuisine* and bourgeois sociability.[28]

Consumer culture's strength derives from its ability to channel and harness deep bodily needs and desires—for youth, health, longevity, beauty, sexual fulfillment, achievement, self-expression, enjoyment, excitement—to the necessities of production and economic growth. These are all true human goods. The problem lies in the hiddenness of a pervasive sense of commodity fetishism and a systematically produced imbalance lacking restraints. So long as something like the institutions of a free market and corporate capitalism remain in America—as they surely will—the only moral strategy which promises any hope remains that of recognition and restraining, tilting the imbalances, correcting for the systematically produced distortions.

There exists an alternative American vision, against the grain of consumerism, documented for us in David Shi's intellectual history *The Simple Life.* Shi tells the tale of the subversion, yet continual reemergence, of the American ideal of plain living in American culture from the Puritan ethic of Jefferson and the transcendental plain living of Thoreau and later in Whitman.

After an eclipse during the gilded age, the quest for a simple life reemerged in what Shi calls "progressive simplicity" with its characteristic practices which right the imbalance in consumerism: "discriminating consumption, uncluttered living, personal contentment, aesthetic simplicity in art and architecture, civic virtue, social service, renewed contact with nature."[29] Both Teddy Roosevelt and John Muir shared William James' fears for an "over-civilized man." After another eclipse in the post-World War I era of prosperity, the ideal reemerged again with the early New Deal's vision of a cooperative commonwealth and the simple life embodied in the youth of the Civilian Conservation Corps.

In our own time, environmentalists and others tap into this persistent minority strand of American culture inimical to a consumerism run riot. Lawrence Rockefeller (of all people!) could write, in the wake of the energy crisis, a *Reader's Digest* article entitled "The Case for the Simple Life."[30]

After surveying the vast expanse of American intellectual history, Shi concludes: "Though a failure as a societal ethic, simplicity has nevertheless exercised a powerful influence on the complex patterns of American culture. As a myth of national purpose and as a program for individual conduct, the simple life has been a perennial dream and a rhetorical challenge, displaying an indestructible vitality even in the face of repeated defeats. It has, in a sense, served as the nation's conscience, reminding Americans of what the founders had hoped they would be and thereby providing a vivifying counterpoint to the excesses of materialist individualism."[31]

Yet Shi does not neglect to note a severe moralistic strain in the American tradition. "Proponents of the simple life have frequently been over-nostalgic about the quality of life in olden times, narrowly anti-urban in outlook and too disdainful of the benefits of prosperity and technology. . . . Too often the critics of American materialism have failed to give adequate recognition to the benefits of modern civilization and economic well-being."[32] Nevertheless, "the simple life, though destined to be a minority ethic, can nevertheless be more than an anachronism or an eccentricity."[33] Indeed, sociological evidence exists to suggest that there is, in fact, a substantial popular tendency to endorse simplicity as a value (to act on it is another question!). Simplicity as a value is endorsed in this country by a majority of two-thirds of the respondents. The people who actually try to practice simplicity may cover a third of the population.[34]

The challenge of a consumer culture to Catholic intellectual life demands an imagination about curriculum and environment in the American university setting which would give students a literacy to recognize the rootedness, pervasiveness and hidden agenda of consumerism (reaching even to how many Americans conceive of love and human relationships, e.g. something they want to consume) and to elicit the moral resolve to restrain its imperialistic tendencies to hegemony. This challenge is unlikely to be met in universities where students consume courses as a way toward gaining access to the class of technical experts and degrees and curricular decisions are based, fundamentally, on market research. Nor will it be met where administrators of universities are not themselves committed to a strategy of deep recognition of cultural patterns and their restraint when in excess.

II. TECHNOLOGY:
THE MACHINE IN THE GARDEN

I have already indicated my distance from anti-technological polemics such as those of Jacques Ellul or from the perhaps wildly utopian schemes of someone such as Ivan Illich.[35] As a social scientist, I have long recognized the implicit technological metaphor in much of sociology. Albert Borgmann points in this direction: "The professed paradigm of many mainstream social scientists in this country is a set of laws that would rival the laws of natural science in precision and predictive power. Why has this paradigm, in spite of its clear if not conclusive failures of precision or applicability, not been abandoned? We may conjecture that the work of its adherents is sustained by another, implicit paradigm, that of getting social reality under control."[36]

There exist basically three competing views of technology in current American intellectual life: (1) technology is a powerful instrument in the service of other values; (2) technology is a force in its own right that threatens our essential welfare; (3) there is no clear problem of technology—it displays an interplay of numerous and variable tendencies. Both position one and two contain some truth. The third position is hopelessly naive.[37]

We need to recognize both the promise and the limits of technology. The original promise of technology was an increase in productive abundance and wealth, the reduction of dehumanizing labor and its replacement by work worthy of human skills and the harnessing of nature and matter toward human goals and for the removal of human ills. No one need subscribe to some Luddite move to destroy the machines or engage in simple fear of them. But no one should be lured to a view that sees the deeply rooted American romance with the machine as simply innocent, value-neutral. Technical rationality and the technical paradigm does take on a life of its own.

There are decisive dangers to our common life in extending the technological paradigm into many or all domains. It has its appropriate, delimited sphere but rarely remains contained there. Langdon Winner notes the tendency to expansion ingredient in the technological paradigm: "The original ends have atrophied: society has accepted the power of technique in all areas of life; social decisions are now based upon the validity of instrumental modes of evaluation; the ends are restricted to suit the requirements of techniques of performance and measurement."[38]

When we make technology center rather than servant of human purposes, we eschew all notion of *telos* and purpose since technology—pure means—knows no ends. "Neither science nor technology has a theory of what is worthy and in need of explanation or transformation. Given an *explanadum* and *transformandum,* they will explain and transform the problematic phenomenon: neither has a principled way of problem stating." For "modern science cannot embody a substantive world view of a scientifically authenticated sort."[39] Hence, technological progress, at its best, can only be liberation *from;* it can never provide us with a liberation *for.*

Technology is linked to consumerism since, in its foreground, the ends of technology foresee commodities and consumption as one of its liberating promises. Moreover, by bursting its proper bounds and domain, the technological paradigm presents problems to modern society in its loss of substantive direction and to modern democracy in its substitution of hard measure economic growth for a "softer" notion of substantive justice and an explicit and definite vision of the good life. Finally, it subverts the meaning of work as a human ideal. "Roughly speaking the reduction of work in technology to a mere means has resulted in the degradation of most work to what I usually call labor," notes Borgmann. The miracle and promise of technology can yield a skewed abundance in what John Kenneth Galbraith calls "a private luxury and public poverty."[40]

Survey data exists which points to considerable ambiguity by Americans concerning the machine in their garden. On balance, the attitude seems favorable but there lurks hidden—because unasked —in most survey questions an assumption that technology is the comprehensive and dominant way in which reality should be shaped today.[41] Technology in our society is rarely offered as something we choose—a way of life we are asked to prefer over others— but, rather, is promoted as the basis for choices. The technological paradigm reinforces both consumerism and individualism. Not surprisingly, when a social paradigm is deeply embedded, we take it for granted as the way our life becomes defined without seeing how it deforms existence.

Jurgen Habermas speaks of a strong segmentation in modern society of the value spheres of science/technology which are governed by purposive-technical rationality; the moral-practical spheres which are regulated by a social rationalization in politics, law, sociology and ethics; and an autonomous sphere of art governed by the rationality appropriate to aesthetics. Habermas sees the modern project as subjected to a tyranny of purposive-technical rationality which subverts the autonomy of the other spheres and forces them into its own technical-rational logic. As Habermas argues in a classic essay, science and technology have become an ideology which colonizes other spheres of society. The imperatives of the larger systems of economy and polity and the scientific-rational apparatus of modern society force their forms of rationality (governed by "success," "efficiency," technical appropriateness of means to ends) on the life-worlds of practical everyday living. Understanding and meaning must yield to success and efficiency. The resultant sense of *anomie,* the failure of meaningfulness in work, family, public discourse, can be overcome, argues Habermas, only by emancipating the inherent meaning and rationality of the other life-worlds from their domination by technical rationality.[42]

The corrective balance to the deformation of modern culture through the technical–rational paradigm lies in embracing focal practice. Alisdair MacIntyre defines the meaning of a focal practice. By a practice, MacIntyre envisions established cooperative human action which can conceive of "internal goods," standards of excellence of a human activity or practice inherent in the activity itself which entails the good of the individuals as well as the good of the whole community. Characteristically, in modern societies only "external goods," i.e. money, status, welfare, power, external success judged by technical standards, count as goods to be distributed and accounted for by a theory of justice.

The notion of focal practices and internal goods is deeply counter-cultural. For, as MacIntyre notes, "the tradition of the virtues is at variance with central features of the modern economic order and more especially its individualism, its acquisitiveness and its elevation of the values of the market to the central social place."[43] Albert Borgmann similarly enjoins the embracing of focal practices as an antidote to the imperialism of the technological paradigm. He urges a characteristic strategy of recognition and restraint: "If there is a way of recovering the promise of technology, it must be one of disentangling the promise from the dominant way in which we have taken up with the world for two centuries now. It must be a way of *finding counterforces to technology that are guided by a clear and incisive view of technology and will not be deflected or coopted by technology.* At the same time such counter-forces must be able to respect the legitimacy of the promise and to guard the indispensable and admirable accomplishments of technology."[44]

Again, Borgmann notes of his reform proposals: "A reform so defined is neither the modification nor the rejection of the technological paradigm but the recognition and restraint of the pattern of technology so as to give focal concerns a central place in our lives."[45] A reform of the cultural paradigm "is even less, of course, a dismantling of technology or of the technological universe. It is rather the recognition and restraint of the paradigm. To restrain the paradigm is to restrict it to its proper sphere."[46] The proper sphere of technology serves as a useful context for but not the rule of and center of life. For technology is blind to *telos,* the proper ends of human action. When it becomes the center of life it necessarily then subverts the proper ends of humanity.

III. INDIVIDUALISM:
IT IS NOT GOOD TO BE ALONE IN THE GARDEN

Robert Bellah et al. take up the probing of MacIntyre in a more straightforward sociological fashion through interviews with Americans about how they see the nature of successful life and society and the meaning for them of freedom and the requirement of justice in the modern, post-industrial world. Bellah et al. demonstrate that the manager and the therapist have become the dominant representative social character types. Managers operate out of utilitarian individualism, i.e. the rational self-interested individual acts to maximize his or her self-interest with hopes that this somehow contributes to a greater good. Therapists see commitments as personal enhancements rather than moral imperatives. Utilitarian and expressive individualism, they argue, are the dominant sociological moral logics in modern America. For the first, moral judgment of alternative actions consists in cost-benefit analysis of competing actions judged by a criterion of external technical success. There are no "internal goods" in any social practices as such.

For the expressive individualist, moral judgment lodges in an intuition of feeling inwardly more or less free, comfortable, authentic. Following the logic of modern liberalism, selves are defined by their self-chosen life-projects which lie beyond the realm of rational adjudication. The consequences for public discourse and democratic political policy are disastrous. "Now if selves are defined by their preferences but those preferences are arbitrary, then each self constitutes its own moral universe and there is finally no way to reconcile conflicting claims about what is good in itself."[47] Bellah et al. agree with Habermas' notion of the "colonization" of the life-world. "Too much of the purely contractual structure of the economic and bureaucratic world is becoming an ideological model for personal life"—for family, friendship, church and local community.[48]

Instead of the virtuous self defined by moral commitments and practices, entailed in free allegiance to a community of memory and a tradition of humane freedom, Bellah et al. find in modern America the socially unsituated self. Instead of work and careers as intrinsically meaningful, a locus for the practice of "internal goods," they discover "mere work" as a source of external livelihood and status. But "the absence of a sense of calling in work means an absence of a sense of moral meaning."[49] Instead of substantive community, these sociologists find in America the "life-style enclave," i.e. groups of the homogeneous, class-specific tribal enclaves, reinforcing group bias and prejudices. But "the notion that one discovers one's deepest beliefs in and through tradition and community is not very congenial to Americans."[50] Neither utilitarian nor therapeutic individualism can carry the weight of sustained and enduring commitments.

Individualism feeds into and off of the cultural elements of consumerism and the devise paradigm from technology. All three are deeply rooted in American culture. All three call for a strategy of recognition and restraint.

CONCLUSION

Adopting a strategy of recognition of the depth and pervasiveness of consumerism, the technological paradigm and excessive individualism in American society and the concomitant moral strategy of restraining their deformation represent a potent challenge to American Catholic intellectuals and their universities. For they will need—against the splintering tendencies of professionalization and the balkanization of the disciplines of knowledge—to achieve a moral unity of discourse and vision absent in American public life and secular universities. But any lesser strategy calls in question why Catholic universities should exist at all as both American and Catholic institutions. Moreover, this unity of discourse and vision will have to be achieved in a manner consonant with American pluralism without becoming a relativism and with the academic freedom appropriate to a university, by persuasion rather than *fiat*. Is it any wonder that the tenure of most university presidents today is so short! Ultimately, we need to go against the grain by working within the culture to subvert and deflect it. Doing so forces us back to the older Catholic wrestling with the meaning of being present to a culture as Christians and the metaphor of the leaven in the mass. Consumerism, technology and individualism define for us the mass. The gospel lived within this mass—not outside it or untouched by it—defines the leaven. Clearly, against the usual American pragmatic hopes and technical-rational imagination, this problem allows for no easy fixes! It is a challenge, however, worthy of giving a lifetime of energy by American Catholic intellectuals.

Notes

1. Leo Marx, *The Machine in the Garden* (Oxford, 1964).

2. David Shi, *The Simple Life: Plain Living and High Thinking in American Culture* (Oxford, 1985).

3. In the *New York Sun,* January 5, 1948, p. 21.

4. Hervé Verenne, *Symbolizing America* (Lincoln, Nebraska, 1986), p. 8.

5. Christopher Lasch, *The Culture of Narcissism* (New York, 1978).

6. T.J. Jackson Lears, "From Salvation to Self-Realization," in Richard Fox and Jackson Lears, eds., *The Culture and Consumption* (New York, 1983), pp. 4–5.

7. Clyde Kluckhohn, "Toward a Comparison of Value Emphases in Different Cultures," in *The State of The Social Sciences,* edited by Leonard White (Chicago, 1956).

8. Cf. Steven Tipton, *Getting Saved from the Sixties* (Berkeley, 1982).

9. John Kavanaugh, *Following Christ in a Consumer Society* (Maryknoll, New York, 1981), p. 56.

10. Kavanaugh, p. 57.

11. Kavanaugh, p. 59.

12. Hervé Verenne, ed., *Symbolizing America,* p. 6.

13. Verenne, p. 16.

14. Verenne, p. 25.

15. John Caughey, "On the Anthropology of America," in Verenne, p. 235.

16. Cf. Albert Borgmann, *Technology and the Character of Everyday Life* (Chicago, 1984), and Robert Bellah, Richard Madsen, William Sullivan, Ann Swidler and Steven Tipton, *Habits of the Heart* (Berkeley, 1985).

17. Lewis Mumford, *The Conduct of Life* (New York, 1951), p. 83.

18. Norman Birnbaum, "The Bishops in the Iron Cage: The Dilemmas of Advanced Industrial Society," in Thomas Gannon, ed., *The Catholic Challenge to the American Economy* (New York, 1987).

19. Richard Fox, "Epitaph for Middletown," in Richard Fox and Jackson Lears, eds., *The Culture of Consumption,* p. 122.

20. Fox and Lears, *The Culture of Consumption,* p. xii.

21. Jackson Lears, "From Salvation to Self-Realization," p. 19.

22. Lears, p. 29.

23. John Hargreaves, *Sport, Power and Culture* (New York, 1986), p. 131.

24. Hargreaves, p. 133.

25. Daniel J. Boorstin, *Democracy and Its Discontents* (New York, 1975), p. 28.

26. Cited in Robert B. Westbrook, "Politics as Consumption," in Fox and Lears, p. 155.

27. Kavanaugh, p. 26.

28. Hargreaves, p. 133.

29. Shi, *The Simple Life,* p. 176.

30. Lawrence Rockefeller, "The Case for a Simpler Life Style," *Reader's Digest* (February 1976), 61–65.

31. Shi, p. 278.

32. Shi, p. 279.

33. Shi, p. 280.

34. For the evidence about attitudes toward technology, cf. Duane Elgin, *Voluntary Simplicity* (New York, 1981), pp. 129–131 and Daniel Yankelovich, *New Rules* (Toronto, 1982).

35. Cf. Jacques Ellul, *The Technological Society,* trans. John Wilkinson (New York, 1964), and Ivan Illich, *Tools for Conviviality* (New York, 1973).

36. Borgmann, p. 75.

37. For a fuller account of these three views cf. Borgmann, pp. 15ff.

38. Langdon Winner, *Autonomous Technology* (Cambridge, Mass., 1977), p. 235.

39. Borgmann, pp. 27 and 29.

40. John K. Galbraith, *The New Industrial State* (Boston, 1972), p. 8.

41. Cf. Todd R. LaPorte and Daniel Metlay, "Technology Observed: Attitudes of a Wary Public," *Science,* 188 (April 11, 1975), 123.

42. Jurgen Habermas, *The Theory of Communicative Action* (Boston, 1984).

43. Alasdair MacIntyre, *After Virtue* (South Bend, 1981), p. 53.

44. Borgmann, p. 153.

45. Borgmann, p. 211.

46. Borgmann, p. 220.

47. Bellah et al., *Habits of the Heart,* p. 76.

48. *Habits of the Heart,* p. 127.

49. *Habits of the Heart,* p. 71.

50. *Habits of the Heart,* p. 65.

American Culture: Reciprocity with Catholic Vision, Values and Community

Monika Hellwig

This conference has included some long-range historical reflection on the relationship between the growing, developing church and a constantly changing, developing, adapting western culture. We have also heard a more detailed analysis of the period since the enlightenment and of the brief span of years since Vatican II when the institutional church became more reflexively aware of itself as a world church and of its relationships with the varied cultures of the entire contemporary world. We have been guided through a consideration of the American church in its cultural setting by an historian, a sociologist, a demographer, and a theologian who is an astute observer and analyst of the contemporary American situation from a Protestant perspective.[1]

The task that remains, then, is to suggest from the perspective of a Catholic theologian active in the American context what pattern of reciprocity there is, and might be, between the contemporary American culture and the Catholic heritage. Two preliminary points need to be made. In the first place neither term of this juxtaposition is simple. American culture, as has already been pointed out,[2] would best be described as continuing dynamic interaction among the cultures and traditions of successive immigrant groups both old established and recently arrived. The Catholic component of the immigrant groups is no longer predominantly Irish-German-Italian, settled in ethnic enclaves and gradually reaching out to integrate with the remaining population. With new Catholic immigrant groups largely Latin American, Vietnamese and other third world peoples, even the Catholic community of the United States lives within the wide range of world cultures; this miscellany is not only without but also within. Moreover, when we speak of

Catholic vision, values and community we cannot assume a mono-lithic structure. Historical survey of Catholic piety, theology, moral life, aesthetic expression and institutional structures shows im-mense variation both in the course of time and across cultures and geographic regions. It is true that a mainstream of understanding emerges from this variety, but the more specific the questions we address to it, the less definite or univocal are the answers that we draw from the Catholic heritage.

A second preliminary point to be made is the following. The interaction of the pluralistic American culture with the Catholic heritage is not and cannot be blueprinted beforehand; it emerges as the product of interaction of free, creative agents choosing their associations, their emphases, their questions, their commitment of energy and time, and so forth. We do make our own history, though we do not make it any way we choose but within the limits and possibilities of the situation which has been shaped not directly by the divine creator but very largely by those who went before us.[3] The immediate corollary to be drawn from this is that it is of greatest importance that we recognize wherein lies our own respon-sibility for the shaping of the future, that we read accurately the possibilities opened up for us by our past, and most of all that we make the right distinctions between what is God-given or divinely decreed and what is fallible human fumbling after the authentically human as enhanced by God's continuing grace.[4] As Christians we are committed to an attitude toward human social life and its multi-ple patterns which is never simply an attitude of acceptance and compliance with what is. Rather we are committed to an unrelent-ingly critical stance which asks at all times what is of the good order of creation, what is of the disorder of sin, and what is of the reor-dering of redemptive grace in the world. Moreover, as Christians we are committed to pursue that discernment without preconceptions as to where the forces of each level of human experience may be at work. There is no basis for assuming that the disorder of sin is not to be found within church structures, nor for assuming that redemp-tive activity is going forward only within church structures or only among believers.

The question, then, concerning the reciprocal relationships be-tween American culture and the Catholic heritage turns out to be a diffuse and rather elusive one to which there cannot be neat answers but only tentative suggestions. Any answers that may be ventured must be less in the nature of a prediction than in the nature of a prophecy that interprets the present as to its meaning and possibilities and that calls for a free response from those who must co-create the future. In that spirit this paper will propose five positive aspects of the American ethos which seem to the eyes of a theologian to offer redemptive initiatives recognizable as such from a Catholic viewpoint. The paper will also propose five negative aspects of the American ethos which seem to call for critique and transformation by the light of Christian faith—a critique and transformation to which the richness of the Catholic heritage seems to have something to contribute.

The first among the positive factors of the contemporary American ethos which seem to me to be theologically significant is the optimistic spirit of enterprise in American culture. As we look about us we see a keen interest in invention, investment, economic and technical development, advances in communication, data retrieval, analysis and all aspects of education and of health care. There has been a subtle, and sometimes not so subtle, tendency on the part of the Vatican to view these aspects of American life and activity as regrettably worldly in their concerns—a tendency sometimes shared in preaching, teaching and writing even by American church leaders, clergy and theologians. I believe that this condemnatory attitude needs to be unmasked as yet another echo of gnosticism in the church. Although we condemned the attitude in the second century, and again in the more virulent form of Manichaeism in the fifth, and once more in the guise of the Cathari or Albigensian heresy since the twelfth century, and then once again in the disguise of Jansenism in modern times, the temptation still haunts us. There is evidently a seductive power in the notion that the spiritual in the biblical sense is to be identified with the immaterial, the a-historical, the other-worldly and the unpractical. Yet in orthodox doctrine the spiritual in the biblical sense is the revitalizing of all creation by the redeeming breath of God drawing all things to their true purpose and focus.

As Christians we confess our faith in the doctrine of creation —one God, maker of heaven and earth, of all that is seen and unseen. The foundation stories in Genesis 1 and 2, on which all subsequent theology of creation rests, place the human person and human society at the center of creation with the responsibility to cultivate the world and its resources, to co-create, to develop the world's possibilities. When the narrative in Genesis tells us that human beings are made in the likeness of God, the only characteristic that has been ascribed to the divine thus far in the story is that of being a maker, an inventor, one who brings forth what never yet has been, a practical imagination. This is the image to be reflected in the human person and in human society.

It is true that the story stresses the centrality of God's wisdom and power at the center of the harmony of creation—at the center of the garden. But that central guiding force is represented as being in polarity, not in conflict, with human freedom and creativity. It is therefore surely a distortion that represents conformity to the will of God as essentially passivity or resistance to change. However, it is clear that something of that type was happening in the mid-nineteenth century when Pius IX issued the *Syllabus of Errors,* and again in 1899 when Leo XIII condemned Americanism, and yet again in 1907 and 1910 when Pius X took such extensive measures against modernism. One might even raise the question tentatively whether the same principle was at work when Pius XI issued *Casti Connubii* in 1930 and when Paul VI issued *Humanae Vitae* in 1968. In any case, all such pronouncements raise sharply the question as to the appropriate interaction of human creativity and invention with divine creativity and the divine will.

A more extensive consideration of the biblical and traditional perceptions of creation, sin and redemption suggests certain clearly discernible criteria for the exercise of human creativity in obedience to the will of God. The most persistent such criterion is certainly respect for the human needs, dignity and freedom of others. To be human is to be a creature that is relationally constituted; a primary fact of our creaturehood is our interdependence with one another. A second such criterion is a basic creaturely humility that acknowledges finitude as practically experienced in bodily needs and limits, in the grounding of intellect, affect and will in our physiological functioning, and most of all in death with its unpredictable timing. Such humility certainly must include a contemplative aspect and a phase of self-surrender, but to be genuine creaturely humility it must also accept the power of creative activity and a drive toward achievement and the mastery of creation's resources and possibilities.

Such enterprise and creativity are to be found not only in technical advances, but also in the construction of society and its various patterns of personal relationships. Thus there has been a spirit of enterprise in communications that favors frank and critical exchange of information and opinion, and favors also a wide dissemination of information that is of public interest. In a similar way, American education encourages critical evaluation in all fields rather than memorization and acceptance on the authority of teacher or text. This has been applied to increasing the efficiency of any business, professional activity or service function. It has been applied to making more widely available not only the necessities of life but also its pleasures and luxuries. In itself this kind of progress is, by Christian standards, a good thing, a practical appreciation of the good gifts of creation including the gift of human creativity. Unless such development of greater resources and opportunities involves injustices, reckless selfishness or actual immorality of any kind, there is no good reason to condemn it as "worldly" in a pejorative sense, as materialistic or hedonistic. Rather the spirit of enterprise, initiative, and creativity that explores and develops the resources of the world and of the universe seems to be an appropriately human perfection to be encouraged and fostered and brought within the understanding of our relationship with God as creatures. And, indeed, it is out of this culture with this attitude that the new strand of creation theology has come to enrich the church's understanding of its own context and foundations, and to correct a certain rather melancholy and passive sense of what it means to be Christian.

A second rather significant aspect of American culture which is or can be a gift to the church is a legal system derived from British common law. It is a system based on "human rights," on the equal standing of all before the law, and on strong rules of due process. A case can be made that these are matters lying very close to the heart of the redemption. Sin, as an over-assertion of human freedom against God, is manifest in self-centeredness, greed and domination. Sin has given us a history full of bullying by those who have managed to seize more wealth or more power, and who have set up systems everywhere in which people do not have equal dignity, equal rights, or equal freedom. They are systems based not on God's good creation but on the bullying power that some have managed to acquire over others in our world. It is the teaching of Jesus that the poor, the lowly, the despised and excluded are the heirs of the reign of God, because when God reigns—wherever God reigns—such bullying patterns are superseded. In the legal systems of the world there has been progress toward this in varying degrees, and it is evident that the British common law system has developed a structure of content and process which particularly assures protection against oppression and injustice.

Issues that seem particularly pertinent to the redemption of the world in the American legal system as it has evolved in our times are both substantive and procedural. Substantive are the rights guaranteed by the constitution and laws, which are based on the concerns with human freedom and dignity that characterized the thought of the enlightenment. While it has taken the church about three centuries to come to terms with the enlightenment, the Second Vatican Council took many positions which indirectly acknowledged the church's indebtedness to that secularizing movement for new realizations of the possibilities of tolerance, of widespread education, for the freedom of the individual and so forth. It is clear that these aspects are prerequisites to a fuller, deeper community among human persons—a community such as is consonant with the reign of God among human persons and societies.

But perhaps the greatest potential contribution of American culture to the church in terms of legal systems is rather in procedural principles that are devised to guarantee justice for all. Such are: the strong presumption of innocence until there is clear and overwhelming proof of guilt; the right to confront one's accusers and cross question them; the right to have issues heard and tried by a jury of one's peers; the right of access to records concerning oneself kept by public authority; the right to insist on the terms of a duly concluded contract, even against employers or superiors; the right to have conflicts tried by the norms of properly promulgated and publicly accessible laws and regulations; the right to hear judg-

ment given and explained; and the right of appeal. These procedural rights and all the implications that flow from them are taken
for granted in countries using the common law tradition, and they
are a guarantee of respect for the dignity of the human person, such
as is required for authentic justice and true human community.

It is clear that these civil guarantees of justice find little echo in
the procedures of the church within its own ranks even today, and
the question arises why this should be so. It can, of course, be
answered in terms of the heritage of Roman law, the essentially
conservative character of the institutional church, the historical
development of the hierarchic structures of the western church
based on secular models of absolute monarchies in the past, the
location of central church authority in the Mediterranean world,
and so forth. Yet none of these contributing factors offers adequate
reason for the maintenance of a system that is patently less just and
less consonant with the goal of the reign of God which is a reign of
wisdom and not of bullying power. American culture has challenged, and will continue to challenge, the institutional church's
legal code and legal system as being somewhat less than truly
human and therefore certainly not a positive step toward the welcoming of the reign of God into the affairs of the human community. To the peoples of the English speaking countries this cannot
but be a scandal until it is set right.

Basic to the very existence of the United States of America is
the desire to move beyond religious persecution to freedom of conscience in religious questions and matters of personal morality. The
pilgrims and pioneers had in many cases experienced the effects of
religious dogmatism and intolerance wielded by the civil power.
European history runs red with the blood of those killed for their
faith and their convictions. By Christian standards there can be
little doubt that punishing and killing people for what they hold in
good faith is not according to the example or the teaching of Jesus,
but rather in direct contradiction to it. Deep in the American culture that emerged, therefore, is the need to take such power out of
the hands of the state and its civil government. Hence the first
amendment to the constitution, enacted into law in 1791, guarantees that "Congress shall make no law respecting an establishment
of religion, or prohibiting the free exercise thereof."

As is well known, the official teaching of the Catholic Church long resisted the separation of church and state under the general rubric that error has no rights, so that Catholic rulers have a commitment precisely as rulers to the promotion of the Catholic faith and Church. The founding fathers of the United States, however, were clearly concerned with rights as vested in people and not in abstractions. Moreover, out of the experience of the plurality of the settlers they simply deduced the imperative of tolerance for the building of a human society in peace. It might be thought that this was simply a compromise, a necessary evil, an interim arrangement to be tolerated while "heretics" predominated, but to be ended as soon as the Catholic faith was widely enough established in any nation. It is no longer necessary to argue against this as an official position because the persevering work of John Courtney Murray culminated, after great difficulties and suffering on his part, in the acceptance by Vatican II of the basic human right of freedom of conscience in religious matters (*Dignitatis Humanae, passim*). The council based its statement on religious freedom on the very nature of the human person as endowed with intellect and will and the capacity therefore to search after the truth in person and not by proxy. This natural law argument clearly corresponds closely to the pragmatic foundations that freedom of religion has in the American experience, though an even stronger argument might be made from the Catholic traditional understanding of faith as a theological virtue in which the assent of the intellect to the self-revelation of God is a deeply reflective and freely willed response.

Yet the fact remains that the theological reasons for religious freedom were not appreciated or accepted by the institutional church until the American experience prompted the critical work of John Courtney Murray, and until he persevered against all official discouragement and reprimand and managed finally to bring the arguments in favor of religious liberty into the debates of the council. This realization prompts some questions concerning the continuing need to press the issue, for instance in relation to the scholarly work of theologians within the church. The suppression of serious debate on religious and moral issues suggests less than full confidence in the freedom and dignity of the human person as foundation for religious and moral discernment, whether it be that of the faithful upon whose experience and questions the theologian reflects or whether it be that of the theologian. There also appears to be less than full confidence in the traditional understanding of natural law and how it is to be discerned by discussion among all persons of good faith. But most of all, there seems to be a failure of confidence in the theological virtues as rooted in the discernment and freedom of the human person responding to grace.

What is said of the work of the theologian might be suggested in rather similar fashion of the discernment of the Christian faithful. Because of the natural law arguments used, the Vatican II statement about freedom of religion has some clear implications for the freedom of conscience of the believer within the church. Those arguments raise the question, for instance, whether detailed discernment of the exigences of sexual and family relations is appropriately carried out for all cultures and societies and for all conceivable situations by one supreme authority in the world, held by celibate persons unacquainted with the cultures and circumstances for which they are making the discernments. The implications of the freedom of religion statement may yet have to be pushed much farther, to apply to the discernment of the living of the faith in changing, unique and challenging circumstances, and more particularly when intimate relationships are concerned.

In a somewhat similar vein, American life and traditions are based upon a deep commitment to freedom of speech and assembly, extended to include the free expression of opinion in the press. This guarantees critical reflection a public hearing even when it comes from groups in opposition to those who hold power, and even when it expresses unpopular minority opinions. How important this is for a just and humane society is evident from contrast with the prior censorship in dictatorships and military governments such as we know all too well in the world today. Repression of criticism concentrates too much power in too few hands. Even if the temptation is only to keep the surface of society unruffled and the machinery of administration running smoothly, the danger of injustice and oppression is great. But our Christian faith alerts us to greater dangers in the temptation to self-aggrandizement, arrogance, conceit, prejudice, laziness and so forth in identifying the corrupting tendencies in unquestioned power over others.

It is clear that freedom of speech and assembly, extended into freedom of the press, academic freedom and so forth, makes the life of any society more untidy, less predictable, more complex to guide and govern. But it is also true that the right to speak out and be heard on matters of common interest and concern creates a stronger, more adaptable, more realistic society, and one consisting of more maturely adult cooperation. And here again is an experience that may be of great importance to the universal church. There are obvious dangers for any society that suppresses minority opinion and silences critics and those who offer alternative policies and interpretations. For a worldwide society those dangers are particularly threatening because an autocratic central authority is necessarily very limited in its access to information and to a full understanding of local cultures and events. Free speech and communication from all who have something to say and free exchange of insights and understanding appear to be critically important to collaboration on such a worldwide scale across cultures of wide variety.

In such context, therefore, it may be worthwhile to point out that continuing efforts in the church to apply prior censorship to theological debate by tighter controls over Catholic colleges and universities may achieve in the long run quite the opposite of what is intended. Instead of creating a more united community with a sound grasp of Christian principles and their expression in a continuing, living, growing tradition, such exclusion of all contrary or critical positions may produce a central authority which does not grow or adapt and is therefore dead, and local churches in which more and more of the faithful drift into open or cryptic schism. The awkward legal and constitutional situation of the Catholic universities and colleges of the United States (as of several other countries of the world) may prove to be a gift in disguise to the church, precisely because in these institutions the principle of freedom of speech as guaranteed in academic freedom is ensured by the secular charters and contracts which govern employment and activity in those institutions.

It is no secret that there are those in the church, including the American church, who deplore the conflict of laws which allows a greater freedom of speech in matters of faith in institutions of higher learning than the central authority in the church freely grants. Yet it may be argued that a church in which the voice of dissent can be freely heard is much closer to the church of the Acts of the Apostles in which the newcomer Paul confronts the authority of Peter and prevails. It is closer to the church in which Bridget of Sweden and Catherine of Siena confront and challenge the pope of their time and win their point, made out of their own Christian discernment. It is also much closer to the idea of the community seeking perfection in which St. Benedict legislates that the community gathered in council shall listen respectfully even to the youngest to hear what the Spirit has to say to the community. There is a basic theological insight behind all these examples: the perfect community in which the reign of God is established functions by communal discernment, not by bullying power or by authoritative voices obeyed because they are such. Only one is to be obeyed absolutely, and that is God. Because all other authority is relative to the divine authority, therefore, there is always a need for discernment, even with church authority. There is a residue of personal responsibility which is not abdicated by a faith commitment within the church.

This question of the ideal to which the church and its life ought to tend in its striving to welcome the reign of God among human persons and societies is closely related to the modern experience of democracy. Again, it is well known that the earliest official responses from the Catholic Church to modern realizations of democracy were not favorable. There was a fear of chaos and even more pressingly a fear that opposition to traditional monarchic structures would necessarily involve rejection of church authority and of faith itself. In the course of time the democratic experiments did not justify this fear, and church teaching came to tolerate and later even to praise a mode of civic life in which responsibility for the affairs of the nation is as widely shared as possible through government by elected representatives.

The early objections raised to this by church authority appear to have bypassed any reflection on the patterns of decision making and leadership in the churches of the pre-Constantinian era. Until the emperors intervened for secular reasons of consolidation of an empire won by military conquest, church leadership did not follow the strongly hierarchic and autocratic patterns that subsequently developed.[6] Indeed, there are strong indications in the New Testament and in the earlier church fathers that the ideal for the Christian community was precisely that of a community living and coordinating its affairs as much as possible by consensus. Even the many admonitions to remain in communion with the bishop in the local church must, of course, be read in the realization that these bishops were not imposed on the communities by an outside authority but were chosen by the community either explicitly by popular acclaim or implicitly as the natural leaders emerging from the group. In those cases where they were designated by their predecessors, this also seems to have been in the awareness of support from community consensus. There is every indication that the local community shaped itself, so to speak, from below. Moreover, there is very clear evidence that not only in the first three centuries but even after the emperors extended their patronage and domination to the churches, matters pertaining to the universal church were to be decided collegially by consensus of representatives of the churches.

What the church of the west lost in the course of the following centuries was reasserted many times in the origins of monasticism and of later religious congregations, and recently in secular institutes and lay associations. Almost always these have begun with the ideal of governance by full consensus and by elected representatives, even though heavy-handed authoritarian procedures may have accrued later. Inasmuch as the religious congregations have always functioned as a kind of contingency plan for what the church at large failed to be or to do, the evidence of this series of new beginnings is very important. It suggests that the idea of true and full democracy is very close to the ideal of what the church is intended to be, and that any authoritarian structures are to be attributed not to the divine element of the church but to its human limitations and sinfulness which make it difficult to escape altogether from bullying power. Scripture resonates with the insistence that the true reign of God in the human community is not by external commands and sanctions but by the sharing of the divine wisdom and the free collaboration of human persons, and the church is the striving of the followers of Jesus, moved by grace, to welcome the reign of God into the world. Because the church is this dynamic toward the kingdom, it is called at every stage of its history to take on as much as possible the character of the kingdom, and that character is one of free persons responding to God's call in their free relationships with one another.

From this line of reflection it would seem that the American experience of democracy as extending to every sphere of life may not be so much of a contradiction of Christian principles but rather a manifestation of them. Not only is this structured and systematic effort to coordinate the public affairs by consensus an achievement of human maturity in the secular realm. It is a challenge to the Catholic Church about its own true nature. It may well be that the continuous discomfort of Americans with the authoritarian pattern of church structures and church life, and the frequent tensions and disruptions that arise from this, are a particularly valuable contribution to the church's long term realization of its own true nature.

The American experience of democracy is unique because of the plurality of cultures and ethnic groupings that must be included, and also because of the sheer size of both population and territory. For this reason the principle of subsidiarity has necessarily played an important role in all levels of governmental organization, as well as in many other aspects of life, and it has certainly shaped the consciousness of Americans in their activities and expectations. They have come to experience this principle as an important expression of human dignity and freedom, and an important aspect of true community in contrast to dictatorial and oppressive patterns of relationship. It is not surprising, therefore, that American Catholics, reflecting on the history of the churches and on the implications of the Second Vatican Council, have begun to wonder why we do not see more local initiative in church policies and actions, why the faithful have no voice in the choosing of their pastors at the parish and diocesan level, and why questions of the orthodoxy of theologians are not referred to consultation by their peers. Such attitudes and questions can, of course, be seen as acts of insubordination to church authority in its present patterns, but it may be wiser to consider whether they might also be a prophetic challenge concerning the nature of the church.

There are also certainly many negative factors in the American culture of our times to which the Catholic Church presents an urgent challenge. Perhaps the most important of these is the pervasive individualism which tends to foster the assumption that any kind of competition for the resources of the world is justified, and that the defense of private property once accumulated is a right that supersedes even the severest needs of others. Moreover, the same strong conviction concerning the primacy and supremacy of the individual is currently manifest in a popularized psychology of self-realization which rejects any obligation not voluntarily assumed, any relationship not found to be satisfying, any commitments no longer experienced as self-fulfilling. While this is clearly a description of the extremest form of individualism, it might be said from a Christian point of view that the whole ethos of individualism calls for careful critique and response. It rests on a conception of human life which is bound to lead to very deep and pervasive frustration because it makes the self the ultimate criterion for choice and action—a role which the individual, time-bound, contingent and relationally constituted, cannot sustain.

There are reasons in the history of the United States for this tendency to individualism. There is the history of pilgrims, pioneers and settlers in what seemed to be an ever expanding land of limitless opportunity. As they were not attuned to the needs of the indigenous American Indians, their harmony with the environment, their style of land use, their sense of communal ownership of land, and so forth, the colonizers must have had the sense that the land with its resources was always there for the taking for anyone energetic enough to clear it and farm it. The virtues called forth were those of the rugged individualist: self-reliance, initiative, hard work, adaptability, willingness to turn one's hand to anything that needed to be done without pre-conceived ideas of class structure or rigid occupational role definitions. Moreover, it is not strange that such early experiences of the colonizers of North America should have resulted in a certain contempt for those who could not compete, who were not successful. Failure and poverty were all too easily equated with laziness, lack of courage, ineptitude, childish inability to stand on one's own feet.

The prevailing individualism might also be traced to the experiences of being uprooted, thrown into cultural, ethnic and religious pluralism, and having to make one's own value judgments and decisions. Under such circumstances, the traditional community patterns do not hold and new ones are not easy to shape. Community support is not readily had, and community sanctions for appropriate behavior are minimal and do not form a close knit system. As modern urban life has developed, people meet one another daily in such overwhelming numbers that relationships are bound to be for the most part quite impersonal. Truly personal relationships are by choice, and outside those choices are masses of people who are seen as personally insignificant, calling forth little or no empathy and no real community bonds. It is a state of affairs readily enough understood as the outcome of history and circumstance, but it is nevertheless a dangerous state of affairs in which the weak all too often go under economically and psychologically.

To this state of affairs the Catholic Church answers with its strong convictions about the communal nature of the human situation in terms of creation, sin and redemption. The nature and pattern of our relationships is not decided arbitrarily by individuals according to their tastes and preferences, but is in some respects God-given. In Christian perspective the neighbor who has a rightful claim on each of us is anyone in need who crosses our paths or comes to our attention. When Jesus proposed this in the parable of the good Samaritan, he spoke in the context of Hebrew tradition in which the solidarity of the people was an integral aspect of the covenant with God as commonly understood. The effect of the parable was to broaden the concept, not to establish it. In the subsequent centuries of the church's existence there have been successive efforts to realize the notion of human solidarity in varying cultures and circumstances, and these efforts have discovered a permanent and inescapable tension: the need to establish a firm common base on the one hand and the need to be open to all on the other hand.[7]

The church of the first three centuries, sporadically but viciously persecuted, clearly saw itself as leaven to transform the whole society in God's own good time. A style of community was developed within the assemblies, and therefore on a purely voluntary basis because no one was forced to join, and this style of community association commended itself on its intrinsic value, which was the basis for conversions and expansion. As is well known, the Constantinian establishment of the early fourth century, while representing in one sense the summit of success, brought with it its own problems. We are the distant heirs to those problems. It was not always clear whether the church had assimilated the empire into a Christian pattern of society or whether the empire had assimilated the church into its pagan ways of domination and respect for wealth. Moreover, this established a symbiosis such that in the conversion of the barbarian peoples of the north personal choice and pre-baptismal years of enculturation were no longer part of the pattern. Even the awakening of the renaissance and reformation did not substantially change that state of affairs. However, with the enlightenment the idea of personal choice on grounds of personal conviction returned.

With the enlightenment also came the notion of toleration of various religious bodies as private associations within a secular state. While this had many advantages, such as the end of persecution for religious conviction, it certainly had the disadvantage of transferring the sense of communal Christian responsibility from the global totality of society to smaller communities of choice. Moreover, there is little doubt that the ethos of the enlightenment also penetrated, at least in America, the believer's sense of the nature of the religious commitment. With the notable exception of the black churches, religious faith has tended to be transformed into its own type of individualism. In many denominations it has not only been reduced to church services, but has been taken much further to minimize even attendance at common worship.

Recent decades have shown clearly what an important contribution the tradition of the Catholic Church can make to the revitalizing of the national sense of community responsibility. With its insistence on coming together for Sunday worship, its renewed efforts to evoke hearty congregational participation, its community building efforts at parish level, traditionally through the Catholic schools and recently through the RENEW program, its welcoming of immigrant groups consisting often of destitute refugees of other races than the locally dominant Caucasian, the Catholic Church has been making a statement about the nature of Christian faith that places heavy emphasis on community responsibilities for whoever may be there and in need. Beyond this, out of the long traditions of the church's concern with the poor and the disadvantaged have come episcopal joint pastoral letters reflecting penetratingly and persistently on social problems and their solutions within our own American society. And out of the universal solidarity of the Catholic Church on a worldwide basis have come similar episcopal statements, expanding and applying practically the vision of world community and its responsibilities sketched in broad outlines in the papal social encyclicals and in the documents of Vatican II, more particularly *Gaudium et Spes.*

We can, of course, be justly proud of the impact which the pastoral letters on nuclear armaments and on the economy have already achieved, and we can see this as the fruit of our Catholic tradition which places such heavy emphasis on the promise of salvation of the world and not only of privileged souls out of the world. But perhaps more pertinent is the consideration that such statements and such an impact depend among other things upon continuing scholarly research that asks the pertinent questions. It depends upon a scholarly tradition in economics that is not swept down the stream of self-serving fashionable assumptions that what is best for the rich and powerful must in the long run be to the advantage of everybody. It depends upon a study of international relations that is not focused simply on the aggrandizement of one's own nation, but is concerned with authentic and lasting peace with justice and freedom for all in the world. It depends also upon searching studies in ethnology and the history of religions, philosophies, cultures and social systems—studies that focus on respectful understanding, not on manipulation and conquest whether military or industrial. It is surely the role of the Catholic universities and colleges of this country to host, sponsor and encourage genuinely altruistic scholarship on the basis of which incisive pastoral guidance and action can be undertaken.

But the prevailing individualism is found not only in tendencies to national and racial chauvinism, and in tendencies to crush the less powerful in the name of free competition. Individualism is found in a pervasive rejection of moral norms other than those formulated out of personal experience and choice. Again, the strong tradition of the Catholic Church in its quest for understanding of the natural law as discernible by reason offers a source of wisdom which the contemporary American culture sorely needs. And, again, it is a role of mediation peculiarly appropriate to the Catholic universities and colleges to pursue in a scholarly way the discernment and demonstration of ethical principles in public and private life which do not rest upon a particular religious affiliation but are closely related to the human situation in which we all find ourselves inter-related and jointly involved. It is a task for the Catholic universities and colleges on the one hand because our Catholic tradition concerning the continuity of faith and reason gives us the foundation from which to proceed, and on the other hand because it can by no means be assumed that the discernment and demonstration of ethical norms for our society is already an accomplished and completed reality, or indeed that it could ever be finished once and for all.

A final dimension of individualism seems to be a growing lack of concern for the future. In public life this shows itself in attitudes toward families with children. The raising of children is presently regarded as a choice that some people make for their own gratification and for which they must therefore pay the substantial penalties. With the exception of a system of free public schools at the elementary and high school level, American society fails to give the support that families with children, and particularly poor families with young children, need in a fast moving, competitive urban environment, and which most of the communist, socialist and moderately socialist countries offer as a matter of course. There is certainly a need in American society for a pervasive sense of reverence for the engendering of new lives, a sense of community welcome to new citizens, a respect for the dignity and the burdens of parenthood, and gratitude for the contribution that parents make to the future of the society. The church has a solid theological grounding for these attitudes, and here again the Catholic universities and colleges might offer an important mediation through scholarship, publication and teaching, particularly in the fields of psychology, sociology, medicine and law.

In private life and in industry the lack of concern for the future shows itself particularly in reckless consumption of resources and in unconcern over damage to the ecological balance of particular places and even of the world as a whole. The assumption that one has a right to use up resources, dump harmful waste, and modify the environment to one's personal or company convenience, and then move on to another yet unspoiled location without assuming responsibility for the long-term consequences, is not uncommon. The burying of nuclear waste for future generations to cope with has become quite customary. The production of acid rain that drifts and spoils lakes and forests at a distance, filching necessary resources from future generations or alien populations in the present has been accepted as necessary for the sake of higher commercial profits. And many other examples could be added to these.

To all of these situations, common sense responds that, left unchecked, they will eventually destroy human life and perhaps all life on this planet. But this is not a strong enough reason for public or private restraint unless there is also a sense of responsibility for the future. Catholic tradition, and indeed Christian tradition more widely, offers basic convictions about human life on earth which ground all behavior in gratitude for creation and a sense of stewardship for the resources of the world in which we are placed. Our doctrine of creation and our eschatology leave no room for arrogant recklessness, but insist that we are the guests of God's hospitality and never the owners of the riches about us. Moreover, all that has been created has a purpose in the divine economy and calls for our respectful and conscientious collaboration in maintaining the world and the universe as an harmonious and habitable environment for as long as the creator calls it and maintains it in being.

This fundamental attitude of gratitude and giftedness which belongs to Christian faith holds the key to human survival and to peace and justice and happiness. But, as all Christians know when they reflect on the matter more carefully, in that state of distortion of perceptions which we call original sin, it is all too easy to focus upon immediate gratification of some provisional desire and to fail to see the larger picture within which a proper hierarchy of values and priorities must be established. Catholic tradition and theology with its frank inclusion of the whole of life in the project of redemption, and its ultimate refusal to draw a line between the sacred and the secular, has a significant contribution to make to a reshaping of American consciousness so that these large issues are not pushed out of view in the interests of the immediate and the individual enjoyment or gain. This seems to be at the very heart of the enterprise of a liberal education—an education for visionary leadership and constructive participation in social responsibility and in shaping public policy, an education for critical discernment and creative solutions to problems, an education for gracious living. But, as we all know, liberal education of this kind is becoming scarcer as strictly professional and technical training take over even in the universities of this countries. The Catholic universities and colleges are among the last bastions of truly liberal education.

While individualism in its many forms is a major negative factor in American life and values today,[8] there are other aspects, among which is the habit of evaluating people including oneself in terms of money—either in terms of wealth already possessed or in terms of earning power. Not only persons but also particular achievements and services to the community are often evaluated in this way. The disregard for parenthood which was mentioned earlier is certainly related to this attitude; by producing and raising children one spends money rather than earning it, and this is seen as a liability rather than an asset to the community at large. But many other activities are not valued proportionately to their service to human life—the work of teachers, of artists, of nurses, of the clergy and so forth. It is not only that they are disproportionately paid, but also that they are considered less successful and therefore subjected to a supercilious and patronizing attitude if not actually to pity or contempt.

What is becoming increasingly plain in American life, especially among the young, is that this puts an intolerable strain not only on those who go counter to the stream and on those who cannot keep up with it, but also on those who are successful in terms of the competition for higher salaries because that competition never stops or comes to rest, more especially in times when inflation is taken for granted as a permanent factor of the economy. The struggle for survival economically is already demanding, but when one's self-worth depends on wealth accumulated or continuing competitive earning power in shifting economic circumstances, the stress is maximal. It is not surprising that we should find high rates of mental illness, family breakdown, drug and alcohol addiction and even suicides. Yet the reduction of personal worth in this way is almost inevitable in a secularized, elaborately technical, highly mobile, pluralistic and densely concentrated urban society. The need for a reinfusion of properly human values and affirmations into such a social context is obviously urgent. The church is well able to respond to this need. Deep in our traditions is the insistence that human dignity and worth before God transcend all considerations of wealth or competitive skills and accomplishments, and that the main purpose of law and order in society is to protect and sustain persons not property, to promote community and not exclusivity. Also deeply ingrained in our church traditions is the sense that cooperation is a more basic and more comprehensive category of human relationships than competition. But these are values and convictions that need to be rediscovered and cultivated at every level of life; they do not come automatically with church membership in the context of our culture, but are distinctly counter-cultural and based on critical evaluation of the prevailing assumptions and attitudes.

Linked, no doubt, with the cult of wealth and power and the evaluation of people and achievements by this measure is a certain deplorable public ambivalence concerning full freedom and democracy for other peoples in the world. There is a prevalent assumption that American national sovereignty excuses or justifies interference even of the most destructive kind in the affairs of other nations for the sake of maintaining American dominance in the world. It is clear that this has, in the course of time, acquired a kind of religious sanction from the tenets of the "civil religion." This religious sanction allows decision making in international affairs on the understanding that the U.S. is destined by God to be an elect savior nation, maintaining law and order in the world on terms which always guarantee American supremacy. Theoretically this role is exercised to bring freedom and democracy to other lands. In practice, as we know from recent events and from distressing revelations about the actual course of those events, there is more often a crude calculation of balancing forces in the world so that the U.S. retains the greatest possible measure of power and access to profit. Like all other empires which began with trading arrangements and then buttressed these with military power leading eventually to a colonial administration of other lands, U.S. intervention is generally based on self-interest assessed in a rather short-sighted way.

There have, of course, been valiant though not always unified protests from church people against the war in Vietnam, against the toppling of the Allende regime in Chile, against various interventions in Central America, most recently against military aid to the Contra forces in Nicaragua, and against such actions as the sale of arms to Iran and pure acts of vengeance like the bombing of Libya. But there is a more far-reaching contribution that the church has to offer, and that is the awareness of world citizenship, of the equal claims and rights of all the peoples of the earth. There is a sense in which the social theory of the modern social encyclicals has progressed far beyond what is generally accepted in the U.S. And this may be because those encyclicals were written in the context of world citizenship with a view to the future of the whole world, from the expectation that all nations are called to be the people of God, living in God's peace and prosperity. The principle of non-exclusion is very basic to the faith and practice of the church. It leaves no room for nationalism at the expense of others, or for any open or cryptic racism that would regard Oriental lives as more expendable than Caucasian, or African poverty as less significant than American comfort.

The plurality of recent and present waves of immigration and the extent of current overseas volunteer programs for young people seem to constitute this a moment of opportunity for an expanded awareness of our common humanity and of our interrelated destinies. The partially successful "melting-pot" experience in which the U.S. has in the past blended into one nation and people immigrant groups from very varied cultural and linguistic backgrounds certainly offers some foundation for realizing both that it can be done and that it is a very difficult human undertaking to bring into a sense of common peoplehood groups that have defined themselves precisely in contradistinction to one another. Humanly we are prone to define ourselves by such distinctions, at the same time giving a positive value to our self-definition by assigning a negative value to all that differs and is alien. The U.S. attempt at this blending has been partially successful, though it has failed thus far to integrate the black population on a basis of real equality of esteem and opportunity, and has much yet to do to integrate the Oriental population of the west coast and the successive waves of Hispanic immigrants from Latin America. Even this partial success, however, seems to have been achieved at the cost of designating foreigners outside the U.S. as lesser beings, and immigrants to the U.S. as people now slowly ascending to real civilization.

This is, of course, with certain adaptations, the story of the church itself from the beginning. The reconciliation of Jew and Gentile, Greek and barbarian, slave and free, not to mention men and women, into genuine community without class distinctions and factions was recognized in the New Testament as a task requiring the special redemptive grace of the cross of Christ. Moreover, it is clearly a task which to this very day is not really complete within the church. Yet, through the efforts of the Christian community through the centuries, and especially through the example of pious movements and religious congregations, the church brings to this unfinished task an ancient wisdom. And for this reason Catholic universities and colleges have a special calling and a special opportunity to approach the topic of international relations and of international institutions such as the UNO, WHO, World Court, and World Bank, as well as proposals for technical collaboration and controls on a worldwide level, such as nuclear non-proliferation treaties, with particular scholarly seriousness, educational persuasiveness, and practical intent.

Another negative aspect in American culture to which the Church has an apt response is one that is rather difficult to define but easy enough to recognize. It is the tendency to reduce substantive issues to a matter of the image projected, a matter of procedure, a matter of public relations. The communist and socialist countries frequently accuse us of colossal waste because we manufacture gimmicks that fill no real need but act as status symbols. And we manufacture a bewildering multiplicity of styles in clothes, cars, and so forth. The endless variety of styles generates feverish production but does not satisfy more real needs. Moreover, it is commonplace that people buying cars in our culture look not to safety features, or durability, or even performance but to the flashiness of the auto body styling. Children learn early to hanker after particular trade marks presently in vogue, and likely to change in a few weeks, for which a shameless increase is added to the price of an article that is no better or more serviceable than the generic item that does not carry the coveted label. We judge our presidential and other candidates for office by ordeal of television, which gives the best chance of election to the candidate who can spend the most money for network time, has had the best coaching in voice production, and the best make-up artist. Very little actually depends on the platform which the candidate lays out or on the previous voting record or substantive character and trustworthiness of the candidate. Similarly, court cases both civil and criminal have come to be decided more and more frequently on procedural rather than substantive issues.

This tendency to take the appearances for the real, the procedural rules for the content, the style for the substance, is obviously self-destructive, but by dint of being very busy, changing fast, becoming ever more absorbed in technology, the country is able to hide the self-destructive conduct of affairs from its own scrutiny. But the university or college is one place where this must not be allowed to happen, and the Catholic university or college is well placed to take initiative in that direction on the basis of the long experience of the church in discerning what is real and what is sham or deceptive. The university has to resist a show of scholarship that is not really scholarly, an estimation of qualifications for promotion and tenure that is based on quantity rather than quality, acceptance of theses and dissertations with showy and unnecessary footnotes or bogus and padded bibliography, passing of undergraduate essays that sprinkle technical vocabulary over the pages without evident understanding of its significance, and so forth. There is a great temptation for Catholic universities and colleges to try to look no different from the Ivy League schools or the great secular universities on various parts of the continent. This is largely a matter of appearances, of peripheral matters, of style that does not touch substance or which falsifies the substance. The Catholic universities and colleges certainly have a great deal to contribute simply by being themselves in the fullest sense and allowing their style to follow their substance naturally.

This true self of the Catholic university or college certainly involves in the first place that it is genuine in its academic claims and activities. Secondly it involves a link with the church, the Catholic faith community, by its interests, its history and its service. It has a great intellectual history, a great intellectual heritage, and it is no step forward to deny this and claim to be just the same as all other institutions. Our history includes a respect for the cumulative wisdom of the generations before us, a readiness to make close links between faith and reason, between philosophy and theology, between speculative thought and practical questions, between the established and the prophetic, between the theoretical and the practical exigence in disputed questions, between scholarship and service, between research and teaching, between matters of justice and claims of charity. Our history also includes a great tradition in philosophy and theology, a sophisticated and comprehensive ethical and legal legacy, a literary legacy, and a finely honed understanding of the relationship of scientific work and progress to the vision of reality that is informed by faith. Beyond that, our history includes eight hundred years of experience of the advantages and disadvantages of various patterns of relationship with the central and local hierarchic authorities in the church.

With all this background and experience, the Catholic university or college in the U.S. has a basis and foundation, not for blindly and uncritically repeating the patterns, but for building upon the past experience with the confidence of close acquaintance with the issues. Certainly our contribution to the American culture must include a presentation from generation to generation of the riches amassed in the past, along with continuing critical reflection and application to new questions and new circumstances. Equally certainly, our task as university is not simply the handing on of the faith in its existing pattern of elaboration, but the analytical and comparative reflection upon it and upon its past development as well as its new challenges and possibilities. That will often mean bringing key questions from contemporary experience and scholarship to the leadership of the church and to the more alert among the faithful. But it will also often mean bringing the wisdom of the church's long life to bear upon contemporary questions in American society.

This links with a final negative aspect of American contemporary culture that should perhaps be mentioned. It is a certain impatience and even unconcern with history, thrusting it aside as though cultures and symbols and relationships and social structures could all be created instantly and changed instantly upon a whim. The eyes of Americans are fixed so tenaciously upon the ever changing present and upon the barely glimpsed but threatening future that hurtles toward us at ever increasing speed that there is a tendency to suppose that any discovery, plan, or proposal made in the past, even the recent past, is already quite useless. We are familiar with the comments made by educators at all levels that young people find the study of history pointless. But that attitude does not begin with them; they assimilate it from the restless pace of life, the preoccupation with change, the social and geographic mobility of society— in fact from us. They can no longer credit any analogy of living patterns, relationships and personal decisions, or even moral values across the generations. This leaves life for many Americans, particularly the younger generations, curiously unrooted, fluctuating, unpredictable. It leaves them unwilling to make commitments for the future, to acknowledge familial and community obligations, even to make definite appointments and to keep them.

There is much in the heritage of the church that offers anchorage and stability. Quite typically Catholicism is built upon a cherishing in deep reverence of the cumulative wisdom of the past, dwelling upon the history of the community, remembering its heroes, treasuring its writings, its rituals, its music and its art. It is important that we share this rootedness in history first with the Catholic population of the U.S. which has not always appreciated it in depth, and beyond that with the country in the broad sense of valuing historical experience as it goes far back through the centuries to formative and transformative experiences and many generations of assimilation and reflection in each case. Here, once again, the critical mediation will be that of the Catholic university and college. Far from stressing our sameness to other institutions, we shall make the greatest contribution by emphasizing our unique, particular history and the traditions and wisdom we have garnered from that history.

To sum up, then, this paper has offered some reflections on the elements of reciprocity that exist or might exist between American culture in our own times and the Catholic Church with its characteristic heritage. This is one particular way of looking at the question, and no doubt others might have made a somewhat different selection of aspects to consider. In any case, it is offered as a basis for further discussion, and for that reason among others I have not been able to resist the urge to reflect upon the particular mediation which the Catholic university or college might play in the reciprocity that was proposed for our consideration. There are obviously many unsolved questions and problems, and the closer we come to practical implementation the more urgent and difficult those questions become, but I have remained with the general principles.

It may be objected to the approach that I have taken here that it considers the church too much on a human basis and does not give due credit to the divine element of the church. This has been a deliberate emphasis, inasmuch as the divine element of the church is its foundation, its inspiration and its goal, which leaves a good deal of decision making, constructing, adapting and so forth to be done by human prudence under the impulse of grace. It does not ask for renunciation of human prudence but for a refinement and enhancing of it. Therefore the human activities of the church itself must come under scrutiny as the times and situations allow. That is why, after all these centuries, there can still be a genuine reciprocity of influence between the church and American culture.

Notes

1. The author had access to the topics and some outlines but not the full text of the earlier papers at the time of writing.

2. Especially in the paper by Sergio Diaz-Briquets.

3. This formulation of the shaping of history is taken from Karl Marx's essay, *The Eighteenth Brumaire,* though of course without reference to divine creativity in the original.

4. Though always basic to Christian thought, this insight has been brought to the fore in our own times by the educational theory of Paolo Freire (see, e.g., *The Politics of Education,* New York: Orbis, 1984) and by the liberation theologians. The stimulus to take human action and responsibility seriously in this way seems to have come from the Marxist challenge in third world countries.

5. Cf., e.g., the work of Matthew Fox, O.P.

6. Cf. Francis A. Sullivan, *Magisterium: Teaching Authority in the Church* (Ramsey NJ: Paulist, 1983); Nathan Mitchell, *Mission and Ministry* (Wilmington: Glazier, 1982); Hans Kueng, *Structures of the Church* (Notre Dame: University of Notre Dame Press, 1966); and the bibliographies given in each of these.

7. Cf. Josef Ratzinger, *The Open Circle: The Meaning of Christian Brotherhood* (New York: Sheed & Ward, 1966).

8. For a broadly ranging discussion of American individualism, see Robert Bellah et al., *The Habits of the Heart* (New York: Harper & Row, 1985), and Bellah et al., eds., *Individualism and Commitment in American Life* (New York: Harper & Row, 1986).

Christians Facing the
Future of Modernity

Hervé Carrier, S.J.

There were decisive moments in history when Christians felt immersed in the agony of a civilization in crisis, yet they had the vivid sentiment that their faith could give inspiration and shape to the culture to come. The great historian of Christianity, Henri-Irénée Marrou, from the Sorbonne, has well analyzed this surprising creativity of the believers in Christ and their almost exorbitant hope of transforming cultures. One has to recognize, as Marrou points out, "the omnipotence of a resolute minority" convinced of being, as it were, the "soul of the world." He writes boldly: "So it is we Christians alone, however unworthy and few in number, who can and must take on responsibility for the world and the direction of history. We alone can give it meaning, implant it within metaphysical reality. I shall quote here the mysterious words which an unknown Apologist flung at a pagan world in the second century: 'Suffice it to say that what the soul is to the body, Christians are to the world. . . .' "[1] Strong expressions indeed, certainly unacceptable to many, today as yesterday, who would accuse Christians of professing an ideology of worldly domination. But not unacceptable to those of us who are convinced that the gospel can enlighten the cultures of the new times, as it did in the past.

That was in fact the persuasion of Saint Augustine, witnessing the end of ancient culture and laying the foundation for the new times. The whole history of civilization after Christ is marked by the leading role of great thinkers, writers and saints whose impact was determinant on the cultures of their times: Origen, St. Cyril and St. Methodius, St. Irenaeus, St. Benedict, St. Thomas Aquinas, St. Catherine of Siena, St. Dominic, St. Francis and St. Clare of Assisi, St. Teresa of Avila, St. Ignatius of Loyola.

It is a similar challenge that confronts Christians today as they are experiencing the crisis of modernity. Vatican II has dedicated one of its major documents, *Gaudium et Spes,* to this question, but we have to recognize that the message of the council, on the church and today's culture, has remained in great part unheeded. This seminar is a proof, among others, that a new sensitivity in this regard is growing in the church. It is hoped that the university world will bring its indispensable share in developing what I would call a new *cultural and spiritual awareness,* an attitude urgently needed in today's societies and in the church itself.

The Catholic intellectual community is facing the extremely difficult but fascinating task of trying to bring the values of the gospel to modern cultures as they are evolving toward unknown forms. Our main objective consists, first, in analyzing thoroughly and understanding the cultural traits of the modern world and, second, in discovering concretely how Christian values can purify, inspire and enrich the cultures of tomorrow. Our real problem is to grasp, from a Christian point of view, what modernity is all about, inasmuch as it represents the typical culture of our epoch.

That was one of the major questions discussed by Vatican II, as the council came to realize that a fresh dialogue with the world of today was decisive for the future of the church. This is the reason why John Paul II, who had been directly involved in these discussions during the council, decided to create, in 1982, the Pontifical Council for Culture. The letter of foundation of this new council starts with these words: "Since the beginning of my pontificate I have considered the church's dialogue with the cultures of our time to be a vital area, one in which the destiny of the world at the end of this twentieth century is at stake."[2]

The Gospel of Christ and Modernity. The central problem can be stated in these terms: How can modern cultures discover Jesus Christ and his message of liberation for the men and women of our times? John Paul II urges all Christians to dedicate themselves with intelligence and generosity to that research: "You must help the church to respond to these fundamental questions for the cultures of today: how is the message of the church accessible to the new cultures, to contemporary forms of understanding and of sensitivity? How can the church of Christ make itself understood by the modern spirit, so proud of its achievements and at the same time so uneasy for the future of the human family? Who is Jesus Christ for the men and women of today?"[3]

How can we, believers, make ourselves understood by the modern spirit? Motivated by our faith in Jesus Christ, we urgently need to investigate what constitutes precisely the culture of modernity. That is the major purpose of our discussion, and it should help us in defining the line of action to be implemented through our *individual* and *institutional* commitments.

In the present essay (a modest but suitable word in view of the subject matter) we shall attempt an analysis of modernity from the *psycho-social point of view,* considering the repercussions of modernization on the collective conscience of our contemporaries, in an effort to discern the spiritual needs of advanced societies, as they are called.

From the outset *modernity* is seen here as a state of mind, a mentality or a *culture* that challenges the church, an approach that was in fact proposed by *Gaudium et Spes.*[4] We must at once admit that the concepts are difficult to pin down and that they carry an ideological overload which can easily lead us astray in our analysis. The terms most frequently used in this connection, "modernity" and "progress," are indispensable but cannot be strictly defined in the human sciences. Insofar as modernity is opposed to tradition, a dichotomy between "modern" and "retrograde" is subtly set up in people's minds, and modernity thus comes to have a normative and idealized sense, since it is obvious that nobody wants to be considered retrograde. Reality becomes confused with myth; modernity is a new and totalizing mentality that involves every aspect of life, personal and social, material and spiritual. These difficulties invite us to approach the phenomenon of modernity through careful cultural analysis.[5]

I.

MODERNITY UNDERSTOOD THROUGH THE PROCESS OF MODERNIZATION

If we are to grasp the culture of modernity it is useful and illuminating to start with the very *fact of modernization,* which has socially observable criteria. This process can be historically identified through its traits and its effects on human societies. We shall try to give a summary of the description of modernization offered by sociologists, devoting particular consideration to the ways in which the progress of science and the technical changes of the industrial revolution, followed by the urban revolution, have affected the spirit of the populations that have been their witnesses, actors and beneficiaries, but often also victims.

Modernization Related to Christianity. We must make a brief preliminary observation of a fact that will be a constant throughout this analysis: modernization is a historical experience that can be explained only within the context of its relationship to a Christian cultural milieu. Modernization is a phenomenon that originated in Europe, and the Christian culture of that continent has provided both a positive and a negative frame of reference. On the one hand, modern science had its origins in the church: we should not forget that Galileo, Newton and Descartes spoke as much of God as of the physical universe. Science successively separated itself from the church, and in the age of the enlightenment rationalist science set itself up in opposition to theology and Christian tradition. Even in the nineteenth century, science was often confused with an anti-Christian scientism. These observations remind us of the fundamental fact that modernization has unfolded in the context of an ambivalent tension with the church. This tension has increased in different ways, according to varying historical and geographical circumstances, and it still constitutes a challenge to Christians, who are not resigned to becoming estranged from the modern world. Today the scientific world, and also the church itself, are in the process of reconsidering more serenely the tense relations of the past, recognizing honestly errors and misunderstandings of both parties. The current revision of the Galileo affair is a typical illustration of this new attitude.[6]

These remarks will suffice to underline the fact that modernity is indeed related to Christianity and remains a challenge for the Catholics of today. We are then invited to examine the features of the modern spirit in order to reach the hearts and minds of our contemporaries. An ethics and theology for modern times have yet to be produced. The observations that now follow have the sole aim of raising *significant questions* for Christian reflection and action.

We are invited to discern the features of modern culture and consider our own position *from the point of view of the Catholic intellectual community.*

Let us start from a sociological description of modernization, and see how it took place with the scientific, industrial and urban revolution in eighteenth century England and then in nineteenth century France. This socio-historical overview is meant to introduce us to the *cultural analysis* of modernity. The advent of modernization can be understood on the basis of *four main pointers,* generally retained by sociologists.

1. The Impact of Science and Technology

In the first place, it was progress in the sciences and technology that made the industrial revolution possible. But the decisive development depends on the move from scientific discoveries to their technical utilization. The sciences transform work and productivity when they become empirical and useful. For example, electrical magnetism and thermodynamics had been known since ancient times, but it was the invention of electric motors and steam engines that marked the beginning of industrialization. To start with, it was simply a question of applying the driving force of steam or electricity to an automatic and repetitive mechanism. Although this invention is simple to our modern eyes, it revolutionized age-old habits of human work. The prodigious development of the sciences of physics, chemistry and biology then led to a rise in the industrial and agricultural spheres that transformed all economic activity and every aspect of life. Technical and cultural changes go hand-in-hand, as we shall see.

The objective of the industrialized world became rationalized and maximized production, so that the economic value of work came to be given precedence over the human value of the worker, leading to a psycho-social revolution that our contemporaries have not yet brought under complete control.

Moreover, scientific progress signaled an increasingly sharp break with traditional knowledge concerning nature and the human being itself. Physics refuted the biblical cosmogonies, and the human sciences provided a new, empirical and positivist image of the human being. Comte, Freud and Marx have had a lasting influence on the view of modern people, both individually and collectively. The impact of this scientific revolution on cultures still requires more accurate consideration.

2. Mobility of Persons and Capital

In the stable societies of the past, people and fortunes used to move slowly, since economic life was to a large extent bound up with the earth. However, everything changed with industrialization. Mobility of persons and capital was one consequence of the manufacturing concentration that soon accompanied a commercial and financial centralization. Fortunes became liquid, and capital was soon in movement to be invested in the nascent industries.

Population had previously for the most part been rural, but now they flocked toward the manufacturing centers, drawn by the lure of earnings. Men, women and children came to sell their labor, but without any clearly defined contractual protection. In a headlong and uncontrolled movement toward urbanization, the first working-class living areas appeared. These were conglomerations of human congestion and overcrowding more than orderly communities, and their appalling material and moral destitution, described by P. Gaskell in England (1833) and L.R. Villermé in France (1840), provided the breeding-ground for the first labor conflicts and the revolutionary agitation of Marx and Engels. In historical terms, modern urbanization was born as a destabilizing element for traditional communities, particularly the family. Apart from this, immigrants to the industrial towns lost their vital link with nature, its rhythms and its regulating symbolism, which are organizing elements of every religiously-based traditional culture, and the repercussions of this loss have not yet received sufficient analysis.

On the other hand, it must be admitted that the city represents a cultural conquest and makes a positive contribution to civilization that should be emphasized. Lewis Mumford is correct when he states: "The city as one finds it in history is the point of maximum concentration for the power and culture of a community. . . . With language itself, it remains man's greatest work of art."[7] However, it is still true that even in the most highly urbanized countries urban life involves glaring contradictions, and we are still a long way from the "intentional urbanization" that would make modern cities into humanly fulfilling communities.

3. Emergence of the Modern State

Another aspect of modernization has been the emergence of the centralized, bureaucratic, representative state. The state came to perform a function necessary for regulating the economic and social activities of groups with divergent interests, but it would become an abstract power, increasingly distinct from society, a phenomenon that Marx and Engels spoke out against as a fundamental defect of modern government which places itself artificially above real society, "creating the illusion that the affairs of the state belong to the people."[8] However we may judge these criticisms, it is undeniable that our contemporaries still have to face a serious crisis in civil authority; they have a confused attitude in front of the exorbitant claims of the state as providence, which tends to become master not only of the law but also of the economy, education, culture, communications, health and demography, not to mention the ups and downs of ideologized politics in modern totalitarian countries. The ascendancy of authoritarian governments in communist countries shows how utopian it is to try to eliminate the state, which Marx considered the flaw of modern nations. In every country the state has extended its power, but in a growing tension with real society. A serious gulf has been created between the political class and living collectivities. The crisis is more serious in socialist countries, although it is equally worrying in those with a liberal system.

4. Individualization of Persons

The rise of individualization is another accompanying phenomenon of modernization. The increased mobility of people and the promiscuity of urban collectivities cut the individuals off from the communities to which they traditionally belonged, the village, the parish, the family. The wish for autonomy exalts the individuals, who henceforth try freely to choose their roles in society, whereas previously these roles were laid down by their milieu, age, family and social condition.

The individual acquires a new status and freedom within society. This phenomenon was brought about not only by the effects of the industrial and urban revolution which progressively took over in Europe, but also by the currents of thought springing from romanticism, illuminism and the various philosophies that preached the ideal of a deeper awareness of freedom and a vigorous proclamation of individual rights. These claims were primarily concerned with the liberation of individuals and called the person to greater creativity and autonomy. These tendencies were notably reinforced by the spirit of Protestantism with deep consequences on social, economic and political attitudes, as Max Weber has later explained. Because of all these reasons, the person acquired a new status in society and tended toward greater self-affirmation. The modern mentality has taken over the positive value of these aspirations to freedom and self-fulfillment, and this represented a cultural advancement which led to the promotion of the person's rights and dignity. Moreover, the advent of the democratic spirit, together with the wish for autonomy, and the mobility and enrichment of individuals acted as a powerful impulse toward generalized education, which is another key factor in social, cultural, economic and political development.

But individualization can also degenerate into narrow individualism. Our historical experience has shown us the tragedy of persons and societies when selfish individualism becomes dominant, leading to sheer subjectivism and the undermining of human communities.

Crisis of Traditional Communities. A particularly striking consequence of individualization is the crisis in traditional institutions and communities. The transformation of the *institution of the family* is emblematic. The family is now increasingly defined in function of the autonomy of the individual at work and in society. The family loses its traditional educational role and its productive and economic functions. It breaks away from the extended family and becomes mobile like the labor market. It limits births, thus striking demography a blow that may prove fatal for the western ethnic groups. The family becomes a "haven of privacy" serving as a shelter for the individual in the midst of an impersonal society.

The crisis of the family is one of the most typical features of modernization, and it has been growing worse over the past hundred years, so that we have reached a point today where the very future of the institution of the family is being put in doubt by the rejection of civilly or religiously sanctioned marriage, the phenomenon of juvenile cohabitation, the rise in the divorce rate, the growing practice of sterilization and abortion, and the spread of homosexuality as a way of life and a new subculture.

If we take the foregoing brief sociological observations as our basis, we are already in a position to attempt a description of the main *cultural implications and consequences* of modernization as they appeared from the outset, with effects that in a sense have continued down to our times and that will affect the developing nations tomorrow.

5. *The Cultural Consequences of Modernization*

When considering the *cultural consequences* of industrial modernization we shall pay particular attention to the following phenomena: (a) a disorganized concentration of workers and their families in urbanized areas; (b) a change in relations between town and country; (c) the separation between workplace and place of residence; (d) an ever-increasing division of work according to trades, tasks and actual types of industry; (e) the growth of a class-consciousness in which workers are placed in opposition to those owning capital; (f) the subjection of workers to an increasingly rationalized production-system, which would later give rise to a feeling of an alienating, meaningless dependence, inasmuch as the worker is compelled to carry out the compartmentalized operations of what Georges Freidmann calls "work reduced to crumbs" (*le travail en miettes*); (g) the setting up of bureaucratic and anonymous relations between individuals, groups and the centralized state.

The *industrial* revolution was therefore just as much a *cultural* revolution, and profoundly shook a system of values that had been secured until then—values such as the significance of personal and community work, the direct relationship between man and nature, insertion in a family that acted as support both in cohabitation and in work, the place of the individual in local and religious communities with human dimensions, and participation in the traditions, rites, ceremonies and celebrations that provided the major moments in life with meaning. Industrialization led to a disorganized, congested overcrowding of populations, thus striking these age-old values a serious blow, without replacing them with human communities capable of integrating and assimilating new cultures.

Never before had the human family experienced such a cultural upheaval and such a traumatic anxiety in front of the unknown, which Alvin Toffler aptly described as a *future shock.* Many times, in history, uncontrolled change had destroyed people, but never had the crisis been so deep and far-reaching in its cultural and spiritual consequences.

The breadth of these changes has set the church hitherto unknown problems in its relations with society and its methods of evangelization. This historical evolution has created the modern world with all its positive advantages, but at a very high price in human and spiritual terms. What will be the impact of modernization in the developing countries?

What Type of Modernization for the Third World? Today when people are trying to modernize *third world* countries they have a better understanding of the advantages of industrialization as well as its risks and its costs in human terms. The experience of the last two centuries has shown that modernization requires certain technical, social and political conditions. Today we must, from the very start, bear in mind the relations between social and economic partners both at home and abroad, and among these partners there are now highly industrialized countries and others that are only in the very first stages of industrialization. Apart from this, it is necessary to conform with existing national legislation and international agreements, such as those of the International Labor Office. These elements come from two centuries of human experience and cannot be ignored. In the light of several decades of development, it can be foreseen that industrialization in the emerging countries will lead to deep cultural changes, affecting individuals, families, local communities and traditions, and that these changes will be no less far-reaching than those that have been affecting western societies since the nineteenth century. It is to be hoped that the *cultural dimensions* of industrialization will receive at least as much attention as is devoted to specifically economic objectives—an indispensable condition if modernization of the developing countries is to be a true factor of human as well as economic progress for the community of nations as well as for individuals.[9] The importance of what is at stake here invites us to carry out a critical examination of the *culture of modernity* as it appears in its positive and negative effects within the historical process of modernization.

II.
THE CULTURE OF MODERNITY ASSESSED

It cannot be denied that modern culture has provided humanity with advantages that no previous period had even dared hope for. Our age feels a very special pride and legitimate satisfaction over the leap in quality and the incredible number of scientific and technical discoveries brought about by modern research.

However along with this feeling of pride and admiration for technical progress, modernity inspires as much fear as fascination. Deep-rooted misgivings are arising.

1. *The Myth of Progress and Disillusionment*

We are now seeing the collapse of an ideology that represented the uncritical hope of the peoples of the western world for almost two centuries. We are witnessing the death of the utopia of progress, which was based on a common belief in the secure advent of a happy society thanks to the establishment of empirical rationality and the final victory of reason and justice.

2. *Rationality Versus Reason*

Rationality has introduced the technical and bureaucratic system that has depersonalized work and most of the relations between persons in social, economic and political life. By a strange paradox the affluent society has brought about a new form of alienation in which anonymous individuals are treated artificially as simple consumers, producers, electors and taxpayers.

3. *Individualism and the Lonely Crowd*

Individualization appears to be both a value and a qualified victory. But excessive insistence on the self-interest and autonomy of the individual becomes destructive for communities and persons. The cult of the individual has destroyed the sense of tradition, undermined the institution of the family and left individuals defenseless within a leveling pluralism.

We note that the cultural pluralism of modern society has decidedly positive effects, but an overly passive acceptance of pluralism entails the risk of destroying people's free choice, while a new mass conformism, an unconsidered consumption of goods and ideas and cultural leveling to the lowest common denomination tend to prevail. These attitudes are disseminated by the "new intellectuals" who earn their living in the productions of knowledge and information. This "new class," as it is often called, constitutes a rising power and is tending to predominate in research, the media and the educational system.

4. *Communications That Unite and Disintegrate*

Social communications should be understood first as a value and a cultural product. The amazement is still with us, a stimulating feeling of universal solidarity and potential co-responsibility for the affairs of the whole planet. The traditional frontiers that had for centuries been so important in protecting national cultures have given way in the face of the irresistible encroachment of the waves that carry the messages, images, advertisements and appeals on radio and TV into free space. Everybody is offered the same information, works of art, knowledge and unlimited opportunities to share in the universal cultural heritage.

This phenomenon is transforming the church itself in its style of communication, participation, information, presence and evangelization.

One of the most notable effects is the birth of a *mass culture* brought about by the standardization of tastes, the universal spread of styles in life and consumption. This results in a *homogenization of culture* and a new form of dominance which tends to be western and American although not at all exclusively so.

One of the most serious challenges facing our era is that of reconciling the advent of a superculture with the peaceful co-existence of particular cultures.

Another effect is the phenomenon of the *socialization of evil.* Never before has the socialization of moral disorder been so universally and omni-presently widespread. Violence, brutality, criminality, hedonism, irreligiosity and professed immorality are vast phenomena to which the whole of society, children as well as adults, are exposed.

5. *Science, a Creative and Threatening Power*

Science and technology have been the driving forces of modernization, and the discoveries of scientific creativity have enriched man forever. But the same technological science that was a triumphant hope and the true creator of marvels yesterday is under accusation by the universal conscience today. Its power has undergone almost unlimited growth not only for our well-being but also for the destruction of man and his habitat. "The data are overwhelmingly clear. . . . Most devasting are those which show rates of soil erosion, desertification, deforestation, species loss, pollution, as well as the fully documented facts on militarization, increasing violence, income division, human suffering and wasted potential. Even if some estimates vary, most of them are more likely to be under than over estimates" (cf. Norman Myers, *The GAIA Atlas of Planet Management,* Pan Books, 1985, p. 259).

What About the Human Sciences? The products of the human sciences are less visible than those of technology, but is their impact any lighter? The functioning of modern society would be inconceivable without the social sciences; however there is a whole deterministic and structuralistic tendency to destroy the humanistic concept inherited from the Bible and the world of the Greeks and Romans.

6. *Toward the Self-Destruction of Modernity?*

A number of recent authors draw the conclusion that from now on modernity is heading for self-destruction. The frenetic race for novelty, superabundance, the search for ever more extravagant sensations, and change for the sake of change will end up destroying modernity.

Modernity and Non-European Values

The cultures of the non-European world have shaken the self-centered ideologies of the west. As Mircea Eliade observed, "The major phenomenon of the twentieth century has not been, and will not be, the revolution of the proletariat but the discovery of the non-European man and his spiritual universe" (*Fragments d'un Journal,* Paris, 1973, pp. 179–180).

Poor Countries and Modernity

Despite considerable and often generous efforts, the numbers of the poor, the illiterate and the hungry in the world continue to grow. This constitutes a dramatic failure of modern culture. Yet fabulous sums and unlimited efforts have been poured into the militarization of our planet. This applies to poor as well as rich countries. Half the people of the world engaged in research are working on war projects. We have reached a suicidal saturation point.

Although this contradiction reveals the most tragic disease of our modern culture, modernity in itself should not be condemned.

III.
RESPONSE OF THE CATHOLIC INTELLECTUAL COMMUNITY

A. University's Cultural Function Today

1. *Cultural Perceptiveness and Commitment*

What the new situation demands from universities, and Catholic universities in particular, is a fresh approach to cultural changes and aspirations, a capacity to criticize and inspire the ongoing cultural trends of modern society. This challenge will require exceptional courage and lucidity. The university institution worldwide is undergoing deep transformations in this new technological and informational age. The university has to redefine its mission in the midst of an unprecedented crisis which is at one and the same time economic, political, ideological and spiritual.

2. *Institutional Leadership*

A creative type of leadership will be required. Daily administration is not enough. What is needed is institutional leadership capable of bringing the whole institution into a syntonic relation with cultural aspirations; leadership which tries to understand these aspirations, learn from them, appraise them, criticize them in the light of human experience and Christian thought. What is needed is the acceptance of *cultural realism* and a *unique cultural role* proper to a university.

3. *A New Cultural Equipment*

Three proposals can be made:

(1) A new attitude is expected—a state of mind able to discern cultural trends often more implied than overtly expressed and difficult to evaluate in their positive or negative elements.

(2) A methodical inventory of today's cultures. Look for typical modes of behavior and in particular characteristic values.

(3) Educators will have to search for points of meeting between the old and the new cultures. Self-criticism will be needed and changes will have to be proposed.

The reformulation of academic aims and programs is in order.

4. *Critical Cultural Realism*

Interpreting new cultures in a lucid and critical manner should rank high among the responsibilities of any university. It should be at the very core of their social function.

5. *The Contribution of Catholic Universities*

The cultural debate we are engaged in concerns not only the future of our institutions as universities, but the future of our society and of our church. What contribution can we make?

The first requirement is excellence through the quality of our teaching, research, publications and our effective service to society. Catholic universities want to be institutions where the cultural aspirations of this new age encounter Christ's message of salvation as it has been handed down to us by the church, living links between the ever-living Christian traditions and the constant acquisitions of the various cultures in the conviction that civilization lives as much from fidelity as from creativity, as much from memory as from projection.

6. *Faith Creating Culture*

The university's cultural mission rests finally on the intellectual and spiritual quality of its *faculty*. Each member of the academic community must be convinced of the cultural creativity of faith. In fact, our faith would remain superficial and rootless if it did not pervade our culture.

B. The Catholic Intellectual Facing Modernity

Needed Attitudes:

1. *Attitude of Appreciation and Discernment*

Modernity is accompanied by undeniable advances in the material and cultural spheres. The church of tomorrow will be built within the cultures of modernity. With appreciation must go critical discernment. Appreciation should not blind us to the counter-values of present societies. We need to speak out against everything in modern culture that is contrary to the gospel and human dignity.

2. *A Cultural Approach to Evangelization*

The stable cultures of the past have been shaken. Evangelization was realized by a kind of slow osmosis. Modernity has given rise to continuous and accelerated change in cultures. Today evangelization requires a much more explicit effort since culture is no more an almost natural ally as in time past. A methodical commitment is needed in order to reach ways of life that are secularized and in constant evolution. The task of evangelization is that of reaching not only individuals but also the socio-cultural environment that inspires them, enriching or damaging them spiritually.

3. *Perceiving the Expectations and Hopes of Cultures*

We must try to discern the *state of mind* found in a society living the experience of modernity. The cultural profile of people reveals their spiritual needs, their fragility, their hopes.

Today we can discern certain psycho-social features of great spiritual relevance. Among these we see:

(a) A feeling of fear and anxiety with regard to the future
  - an elementary philosophy and a radical search for human survival
  - an ontological crisis—not simply a crisis of morals or of atheism or agnosticism; what is at stake is the human being as such
  - an immense thirst and search for meaning and for ultimate motivations
(b) Overcoming fatalism
  - a feeling of powerlessness in the face of infinitely complex problems
  - a need to proclaim the firm conviction that we can in fact regain control of our future by a moral and spiritual upsurge
(c) A universal search for justice and peace
  - discovering interdependence
  - realizing that the co-existence of extreme poverty and ostentatious affluence is a scandal
  - a yearning for unity, peace and co-responsibility with freedom and respect for all

(d) The rise of new cultures
  - attention to the values being sought especially by the younger generation and the newer nations
  - a striking search for religious experiences
  - increased awareness of the fact that each person has his/her own dignity and rights

(e) The new relationship between women and men
  - a cultural turning point of historic importance; one of the deepest cultural changes of our day.
  - the search for a new condition of women within modern society

Reconciling the Two Faces of Culture. Our discussions on the future of modernity cannot lead us yet to any satisfying conclusions, but they invite us to further reflection and joint research among ourselves in an ecumenical spirit and in cooperation with all persons of good will.

What we see more clearly, I think, is that we have to broaden our usual way of trying to influence cultures. In general, we are more at ease when we deal with the intellectual and aesthetic side of culture. We are more familiar with the method of influencing cultures through ideas, scientific invention and artistic creativity. Our traditional intellectual approach still retains all its validity, of course, since ideas and philosophies do make a difference and do change cultures. But a different and complementary approach is now revealing itself to be necessary. Analyzing philosophical systems and their influence on society remains indispensable, but we see more clearly today the urgency of studying cultures as specific realities generating new ways of living, thinking, behaving.

In other words, we are becoming more sensitive today to the *anthropological side* of cultures, influenced not only by intellectual thought but also by the revolution of values, sentiments and mentalities. Cultures are deeply transformed in modern society by the human impact of the worldwide phenomena of industrialization, urbanization, mass communications, global interdependence and the universal hope for a just world. This being so, our cultural action will take on a new dimension. We will try to analyze the dominant life-styles around us, criticizing them, and to find new ways to act on the key-values that give form to cultures.

Of course, our action will predominantly remain on the educational level, in training minds and consciences, but we will also teach to the young generations that the culture of tomorrow depends on their common discernment, joint effort and ability to mold cultural reality as such.

This is a fascinating challenge for Christian intellectuals. Their response might be decisive in reminding our contemporaries that, provided we all join forces, there will be hope of giving a human face to tomorrow's form of modernity.

Notes

1. Henri-Irénée Marrou, *Crise de notre temps et réflexion chrétienne (de 1930 à 1975)* (Paris, Editions Beauchesne, 1978). See his "Une civilisation d'inspiration chrétienne," pp. 41–53, his classic study *Saint Augustin et la fin de la culture antique* (Paris, 1958, 4th ed.), and also his essay *St. Augustine and His Influence through the Ages* (London, 1957). Vatican II used several times the image of the Christians as "the soul of human society": see *Gaudium et Spes,* n. 40; *Lumen Gentium,* n. 38, which quotes *Epist. ad Diognetum,* n. 6.

2. Autograph Letter for the foundation of the Pontifical Council for Culture, May 20, 1982, *A.A.S.* 74 (1983), 683–688.

3. John Paul II to the Pontifical Council for Culture, January 15, 1985.

4. *Gaudium et Spes,* nn. 4–10. The working definition of *culture* we are adopting is the one used by *Gaudium et Spes,* n. 53. I have discussed the modern relevance of that definition in my paper "Understanding Culture: The Ultimate Challenge of the World Church?" in J. Gremillion (ed.), *The Church and Culture since Vatican II: The Experience of North and Latin America* (Notre Dame: University of Notre Dame Press, 1985), pp. 13–30.

5. For a review of current methods in cultural analysis, see R. Wuthnow, J. Hunter, J.D. Bergesen, and E. Kurzweil, *Cultural Analysis* (London, Boston: Routledge and Kegan Paul, 1984).

6. Paul Cardinal Poupard (ed.), *Galileo Galilei: Toward a Reso-*

lution of 350 Years of Debate, 1633–1983 (Pittsburgh: Duquesne University Press, 1987).

7. Lewis Mumford, *The Culture of Cities* (New York: Harcourt, Brace and Co., 1938), p. 3.

8. K. Marx, *A Contribution to the Critique of Political Economy* (first published in Berlin, 1859).

9. This ethical and cultural approach to development is firmly stressed in the recent encyclical of John Paul II, *Sollicitudo Rei Socialis,* December 30, 1987. An analogous approach is adopted by the "World Decade of Cultural Development" decided by the United Nations for 1988–1997.

Reflections on the Protestant Experience

Martin E. Marty

I.

"PRESENT AT THE CREATION:"
A COVENANTED CULTURE (1607–1776)

When people of Protestant heritage or disposition look at the cultural artifacts, including those connected with higher education, in the United States, they have instincts which connect their faith with the culture. They were, as an old saying and a book title have it, "present at the creation," so to speak.

The creation involved the settlement, largely by Protestant people, of thirteen colonies. Many of these were founded on "federal" (*foedus* = covenant) lines. When independence came, there may have been only 30,000 Roman Catholics and 3,000 Jews in these colonies' population. Of course, native Americans and the imported blacks did not count.

Mircea Eliade has pointed out that the commitment which goes with settlement implies consecration. So the evangelical Protestant lineage sees itself as the consecrators of the original colonies, and consecrated by their experience. They used biblical language to interpret their errand into the wilderness, their being a new Zion in America, their prospect of the kingdom of God. It is hard to sever religion, Protestant religion, from law or education or other major dimensions of colonial culture.

Protestant reflection suggests that a particular kind of Protestantism dominated. This was not Lutheran, with its "paradoxical" (as H. Richard Niebuhr properly would have it) relation to culture. No, through Puritans, Dutch Reformed, even Anglicans, it was somehow Calvinist. There was strong faith in natural law and common grace, and (H. Richard Niebuhr again had it right) the motif was that Christ was always "transforming culture"; his people were bringing in the kingdom of God.

The central theme, the bedrock ideas (Ortega y Gasset called them *creencias*), came out of their motif. They were an elect people, chosen for a mission and a destiny, given a personal and corporate vocation, pushed toward a destiny, a light to the nations, a city set upon a hill. An inner tension developed between the Protestant covenantalism, which is corporate, and the Protestant individualism, which introduced intense (also economic) competition.

For Protestants this colonial culture meant that ecclesial events affected the whole community. Thus the conversions during the great awakening of the 1730s and 1740s implied that the larger culture had something at stake in the building up of revivalist churches and revived people. Yet there was also tension between this and the distinctively modern notion that the individual "chooses" to be converted or not, "decides" whether to respond to revival, "picks and chooses" the church which best ministers to need or calls forth commitment.

For outsiders, "all others," those marginal to the culture—Catholics, Jews, Indians, blacks, dissenters, traders, commercial elites—this status meant that they were marginalized. They had to protest, adapt, feel or be second class, or disappear. Among other things, it meant that only a few small Catholic institutions in Maryland could be started.

The cultural context meant much for higher education. Protestant word-centeredness meant that verbal propagation of culture was favored, over against iconic or gestural versions. Literacy received a high premium: hence, Harvard, Yale, College of New Jersey, Dartmouth, even the Baptist dissenters' Brown, became citadels of "covenanted" culture. Yet they were not sectarian or otherworldly; they were not, like twentieth century fundamentalist schools, withdrawn "Bible colleges." They insisted upon and trusted liberal arts education from the beginning. The "Christ transforming culture" motif allowed for culture to compromise Christ at the same time; hence, with these foundings came a high potential for various forms of secularization or religious change.

The legacy of this "covenanted" concept was a semi-secular version of "Christ transforming culture." Catholics have found it possible to relate to this culture of "Protestantdom" with its analogues to "Christendom," middle ages style, better than some modern Protestants can do.

II.

PARTNERS IN INVENTING A FEDERAL REPUBLIC (1776–1791)

The summary event of the new period was the achievement of independence, along with the drafting and ratifying of the constitution. This was the time of early nation building.

Again, Protestants were focal, but their elites were of new character. Most remained church members, but favored what Henry May calls the "moderate enlightenment." They were quasi-Deists more than biblical theists. But they could form coalitions with sectarians who, with enlightenment figures, came to resist church establishment as a means of bonding Christ and culture. The result was the first amendment, which solved the religious problem by not solving it, but relocating it as "a private affair."

The central theme that had a bearing on all culture was now the founding not of a covenant but a "large federal republic" (James Madison), which assured freedom for and helped blunt negative efforts of "factions, interests, and sects" (*Federalist Papers*). These may be "adverse to the permanent and aggregate interests of the Republic," but they will not go away, should not be legally destabilized, and can make positive contributions.

Again there was a tension within the federal situation. John Jay in *Federalist II* gloried in that culture which resulted from "a people descended from the same ancestors, speaking the same language, professing the same religion, attached to the same principles of government, very similar in manners and customs." James Madison in *Federalist X and LI* insisted that "in a free government the security of civil rights must be the same as that for religious rights. It consists in the one case in the multitude of interests, and in the other in the multiplicity of sects." Now religion was free, but it was relocated and had a charter for true pluralism.

This all meant for Protestants that officially no one party of influence or interpretation could dominate. Churches are legally subordinate, but more free to propagate when they were in coordinated positions (as establishments) in many colonies. For others, it meant that the legal charter for future free development was here. There were enormous gains to which these once-outsiders could ever after appeal. For Catholics, the alliance was easy, since the moderate enlightenment was also congenial to natural law thinking. Catholics could by no means always agree with Protestant interpretations of special revelation, but they could at least debate with non-Catholic enlightenment "natural law" thinkers. They were "at home" in this America.

For higher education, religion had become a problem. Thomas Jefferson and James Madison did not know quite what to do with religion as "opinion," which could not be coerced, or as "superstition," which could blight education. They marginalized it at their University of Virginia. Benjamin Franklin, however, as early as 1749 spoke of a generalized "publick religion" as being necessary for the development of private character and public virtue. He did not favor most religion of most churches, and found that their doctrines conflicted and they cancelled each other out on some terms. But they also promoted a valuable, usable common morality.

The legacy in higher education was the charter for religious colleges; they were licit, not to be disabled; they were not to be privileged nor would their meaning-systems have legally based monopoly or hegemony. There was now freedom of choice among collegia, ecclesiae, and world views.

III.

DOMINATING A VOLUNTARY SOCIETY (1791 TO 1945FF.)

Protestant reflection next turns on the long "national period," viewed first as a kind of Protestant empire. The summary event was the "filling up" of first frontier and then urban America, the developing of its cultural institutions on a voluntary basis.

Again we ask, "which Protestants" dominated? The old stock tried to retain power; the Anglo and Scotch-Irish often disfavored those of continental stock, though they could coalesce (as in an Evangelical Alliance, after 1846). Now a generalized evangelical coalition and ethos dominated the culture, in a style that mixed defensiveness and aggressiveness against "outsiders" within. There developed what I call a "federal center" of churches, symbolized by those who in 1908 formed a Federal Council of Churches (without Catholics, sectarians, extreme conservative Protestants).

The central theme now became the retention of what Robert Handy called "a Christian America, Protestant style," what Ernest Tuveson saw as a "redeemer nation," or what I called, in another book title, a "righteous empire." This was a period in which enormous energies were loosed to build reform movements, to propagate the Protestant message and way of life, to shape what Alexis de Tocqueville called the *moeurs,* the mores, the "habits of the heart" and summary ideas of the culture.

For Protestants this self-chosen responsibility meant a time of cultural creativity in churches, legislation, and voluntary associations, though least of all in the arts. Now came Nativism, the Ku Klux Klan, the American Protective Association, and, as a last gasp, the anti-Catholic Protestants and Other Americans United for Separation of Church and State.

For those against whom these united, this cultural situation meant ambivalence and confusion. They were free to influence, but frustrated in many attempts. As late as 1927 an astute French visitor, Andre Siegfried, could still observe that America was a Protestant nation; it had a Protestant culture.

For higher education, the new situation put Protestants, Catholics, and others on the same level: they could start and support their own colleges. There they could cultivate their separate meaning-systems and worldviews. But they were eclipsed by the rise of (necessarily more or less secular) tax-supported state schools and by differentiated and specialized graduate education. There religion, already a private and sectarian affair in the public eye, was further boxed in. The result? Excellent denominational colleges, shadowed by new forces.

The legacy from this era is the system of religiously connected colleges which contribute to the common culture but were free to develop separate identities and meaning systems. Most of these evangelicals kept building liberal arts colleges, not Bible colleges; Catholics favored similar liberal arts models.

IV.

UNCERTAINTY OVER STATUS IN
PLURALIST SOCIETY (1830s TO 1950s)

Summary events in this overlapping period included the mass immigration of other peoples, with other languages, other religions. There was a growing articulation and self-consciousness: the "center does not hold." From west came non-Protestant Asians; from east and south, Africans; from east and north, also secularized Europeans; from the center, native Americans. These all challenged Protestantdom, white-style.

Meanwhile, there was schism in the ranks of the Protestant custodians of culture. The "liberal/moderate" mainstream became divorced from the Protestant right wing. Both saw a menace in Catholicism and secularism, but the moderates gradually yielded space to the former and affirmed, adapted to, and became friendly with the latter. The fundamentalist reactionaries tended to seek the *restitutio ad integrum,* a going back to the "fundamentals," also in Protestant visions of statecraft and moral influence.

The central theme involved the moderates and liberals in efforts to move beyond "mere" or "utter" pluralism to a kind of civil or civic pluralism, which must seek some kind of coherence. The seekers of the old homogeneity among the reactionaries, however, craved the old Protestant Christian America.

This all meant progressive displacement from cultural centrality among old-line Protestants. They did not disappear, and even knew period churchly prosperity. But the voice was muffled in the culture, seen as unrepresentative of anything but its bureaucratic leadership.

For others it all meant a move beyond being subjects of tolerance to acquiring true status in pluralist America. When Protestants were insecure, they experienced inconvenience, harassment; at other times, the formerly marginalized Indians, blacks, women, Catholics, and others were or became secure contributors to the pluralist culture's diffuse mainstream.

For higher education the new situation was confusing. It meant a diffusion of energies and voices. How did the "many" colleges with many outlooks relate to the "one" that was to be the Republic? The colleges were free to make specific Christian, e.g. Catholic, contributions. If they "went too far" in cultural exposure, they often lost their core and blended in. If they "stayed too far back," they lost the ear of the culture. They were at a very busy crossroads, in a complicated zone of culture.

Protestant reflection ends, then, with a glance at the present moment. Today life is lived between the dream of the "unum," of sameness, of at least minimal coherence and consensus on the one hand as subcommunities relate to the larger community, and a "dug-in" pluralism on the other. On that hand are sectarianisms based on everything from Protestant conservative reaction to secularist defensiveness and unwillingness to listen.

There are signs, however, that today in ecumenical, interfaith, semi-secular, semi-religious America, alert academics are finding new ways to be heard. The voice of religion is more manifest than it was in the recent past, in debates over the public philosophy, polity, education, healing, and the like. The church-related institution of higher learning is thus a small element in the academic economy, but an important locale for stating alternative visions of life in the various central zones of culture. It is a time which will demand the best brains, much energy, and a willingness to hear and speak up.